A HISTORY OF BALLET AND DANCE

A HISTORY OF BALLET AND DANCE

in the Western World

Alexander Bland

BARRIE & JENKINS
COMMUNICA-EUROPA

Facing title page: three dancers. Drawing by Pablo Picasso, 1920

First published in 1976 by
Barrie & Jenkins Limited
24 Highbury Crescent, London N5 1RX

Reprinted 1978

© 1976 Alexander Bland

This book was designed and produced in Great
Britain by London Editions Ltd, 30 Uxbridge
Road, London W12 8ND

ISBN 0 214 20283 6

Printed and bound in Italy

To the one who has danced with most spirit

Inscription on a Greek cup, *c.* 500BC

Dancer. After a drawing by Vaslav
Nijinsky, 1919

Contents

Chronology

In the following chronology, stage performances (ballets, operas, plays) are printed in italics, titles of books and paintings within quotation marks.

BC

c. 3500	Saharan rock-paintings of dancers
c. 2500	Painted and carved images of Egyptian dancers
c. 1500	Indian bayadère dances introduced into Egypt
c. 1400	Destruction of Knossos in Crete
1350	Death of Tutankhamen
c. 1175	Siege of Troy
c. 600	Festivals of Dionysus established at Athens
c. 500	Thespis introduces an actor into festival performances
480	Persians defeated by the Greeks at Salamis
456	Death of Aeschylus
424	Death of Herodotus
407	Death of Euripides
406	Death of Sophocles
404	Sparta dominates all Greece
380	Death of Aristophanes
364	Etruscans dancing in Rome
348	Death of Plato
300	Foundation of Artists of Dionysus Guild
146	Greece annexed by Rome
63	Augustus becomes Emperor
c. 50	Bathyllus and Pylades dancing in Rome

AD

c. 22	Pantomime mania in Rome
54	Nero becomes Emperor
c. 150	Death of Lucian
c. 300	Longus' 'Daphnis and Chloe'
354	Birth of St Augustine
410	Rome sacked by the Goths
814	Death of Charlemagne
c. 1280	'Le Roman de la Rose'
1321	Death of Dante
1393	Le Bal des Ardents
1416	'De Arte Saltandi' by Domenico di Piacenza
1453	Fall of Constantinople
1463	'De Practica seu Arte Tripudii' by Guglielmo Ebreo
1465	'Il Libre dell'Arte del Danzare' by Antonio Cornazano
1477	Louis XI becomes king of all France
1490	Ball at wedding of Catherine of Aragon and Prince Arthur of England
	Leonardo da Vinci designs festival for Duke of Milan
1492	Discovery of the New World
1504	Leonardo's 'Mona Lisa'
1533	Catherine de Medici marries Henri II of France
1545	Serlio's 'Second Livre de la Perspective'
1558	Elizabeth becomes queen of England
1564	Death of Michelangelo
1573	Le Balet des Polonais
1580	First proscenium theatre built in Italy
1581	Le Balet Comique de la Royne Louise
1588	Arbeau's 'Orchésographie'
1601	Shakespeare's Hamlet
1605	Cervantes' 'Don Quixote'
1626	Louis XIII dances in La Douairière de Billebahaut
1638	Niccola Sabbatini's 'Manual for Constructing Theatrical Scenes'
1645	Joseph Furtennbach's 'Architectura Recreationis'
1649	Execution of Charles I of England
1653	Louis XIV dances as the Sun King in Le Balet de la Nuit
	Gian Battista Lulli appointed Master of Royal Music in Paris
1660	Death of Velasquez
1661	Foundation of Académie Royale de la Danse
1664	Lully collaborates with Molière
1669	Foundation of Académie Royale de la Musique
1677	Racine's Phèdre
1681	The first girl dances in the Paris Opéra
1689	Purcell's Dido and Aeneas
1699	Feuillet's Choréographie
1703	St Petersburg founded by Peter the Great
1712	John Weaver's 'Essay towards a History of Dancing'
1713	Ballet School set up at the Paris Opéra
1717	Weaver's The Loves of Mars and Venus, a ballet d'action
1725	Pierre Rameau publishes Le Maître à Danser
1738	Ballet School set up at St Petersburg
1740	Frederick the Great becomes King of Prussia

1748	Gaetan Vestris joins the Paris Opéra	1896	Tchekov's *The Seagull*
1750	Hilferding ballet-master in Vienna	1900	Isadora Duncan dances barefoot in Paris
1755	Noverre watches Garrick act at Drury Lane, London	1906	Diaghilev organizes exhibition of Russian Art in Paris
1760	Noverre's 'Lettres sur la Danse' published in Stuttgart		Death of Cézanne
	Rousseau's 'La Nouvelle Héloïse'	1907	Picasso paints 'Les Demoiselles d'Avignon'
	Angiolini ballet-master in Vienna	1908	Diaghilev organizes season of Russian opera in Paris
1762	Catherine becomes Empress of Russia	1909	Diaghilev launches his Ballets Russes in Paris
1772	Début of Auguste Vestris at the Paris Opéra	1910	Fokine's *Schéhérazade* and *The Firebird*
	Diderot's 'Encyclopédie'	1911	Fokine's *Petrushka*
1773	Maximilien Gardel dances at the Paris Opéra unmasked	1912	Fokine resigns from Ballets Russes
1776	American Declaration of Independence		Nijinsky's *L'Après-midi d'un Faune*
1786	Galeotti's *The Whims of Cupid and the Balletmaster*	1913	Nijinsky's *Le Sacre du Printemps*
1789	Dauberval's *La Fille Mal Gardée* at Bordeaux	1914	World War I
	French Revolution	1916	Martha Graham enters St Denis-Shawn school in Los Angeles
1791	Death of Mozart	1917	Russian Revolution
1796	Didelot's *Flore et Zéphire* at the King's Theatre. London		Nijinsky dances for last time, in Buenos Aires
1808	Goethe's 'Faust'		Picasso designs *Parade* for Ballets Russes, choreography by Massine
1812	Vigano ballet-master in Milan	1920	Ballets Suédois founded by Rolf de Maré
1816	Rossini's *The Barber of Seville*		Foundation of Royal Academy of Dancing in London
1819	Géricault's romantic painting 'The Raft of the "Medusa"'	1921	Diaghilev's *The Sleeping Princess* at the Alhambra, London
1820	Blasis's 'Theory and Practice of Dancing'	1924	Balanchine defects from Russia
1824	Delacroix's 'The Massacre at Chios'	1926	Frederick Ashton's *Tragedy of Fashion*, Puccini's *Turandot*
1827	Death of Beethoven	1928	Balanchine's *Apollon Musagète* for the Ballets Russes
1828	Blasis's *The Code of Terpsichore*	1929	Diaghilev dies in Venice
1829	August Bournonville ballet-master in Copenhagen	1930	Ballet Rambert founded in London
1830	Victor Hugo's *Hernani*	1931	Death of Pavlova
1831	Meyerbeer's opera *Robert le Diable* with Marie Taglioni		Sadlers Wells Ballet founded in London
1832	Taglioni's *La Sylphide*	1932	Ballets Russes de Monte Carlo founded
1834	Elssler's début in Paris	1934	Fonteyn joins the Sadlers Wells Ballet
1837	Blasis director of Dance Academy in Milan		Tudor's *The Planets* for Ballet Rambert
1839	Berlioz's 'Roméo et Juliette'	1939	World War II
	Maywood's début in Paris		American Ballet Theatre founded in New York
1840	Elssler tours America	1940	Lavrovsky's *Romeo and Juliet* for Kirov Ballet
1841	Coralli's and Perrot's *Giselle*	1942	Death of Fokine
1842	Perrot joins Her Majesty's Theatre, London	1944	Robbins' *Fancy Free* for American Ballet Theatre
1845	*Pas de Quatre* at Her Majesty's theatre, London	1945	Ballets des Champs Elysées founded in Paris
1847	Marius Petipa invited to Russia	1946	Sadlers Wells Ballet moves to Covent Garden
1857	Baudelaire's 'Les Fleurs du Mal'	1948	New York City Ballet founded
1862	Petipa becomes ballet-master in St Petersburg	1950	London Festival Ballet founded
	Petipa's *Pharaoh's Daughter*		Death of Nijinsky
1865	Wagner's *Tristan and Isolde*	1951	Canadian National Ballet founded
1866	Tolstoy's 'War and Peace'	1956	Sadlers Wells Ballet becomes the Royal Ballet
	Dostoevsky's 'Crime and Punishment'	1960	Béjart director of ballet in Brussels
1867	Marx's 'Das Kapital'	1961	Dutch National Ballet founded
1869	Petipa's *Don Quixote* in Moscow		Nureyev defects from Russia
1870	Saint-Léon's *Coppélia* in Paris		Cranko director of Stuttgart Ballet company
	Napoleon III defeated by Prussia at Sedan	1962	Australian Ballet founded
1874	First Impressionist Exhibition in Paris	1963	Ashton director of Royal Ballet
	Mussorgsky's *Boris Godunov*	1964	New York City Ballet moves to Lincoln Center
1877	Petipa's *La Bayadère* in St Petersburg	1967	London Contemporary Dance Theatre founded
	Swan Lake, choreographed by J. Reisinger, flops in Moscow	1970	Makarova defects from Russia
	Verdi's *Otello*		MacMillan director of Royal Ballet
1890	Petipa's *The Sleeping Beauty* in St Petersburg	1973	Baryshnikov defects from Russia
	Van Gogh shoots himself	1976	Fiftieth anniversary of Martha Graham Company
1892	Ivanov's *The Nutcracker* in St Petersburg		Fiftieth anniversary season of Ballet Rambert
1893	Death of Tchaikovsky		
1895	*Swan Lake*, choreographed by Petipa and Ivanov, in St Petersburg		

I
A PAGEANT OF DANCING

Wall painting of masked dancers at
Tanzoumaitak, Algeria. Prehistoric

The universe can truthfully be described as a compendium of choreography, a gigantic ballet in which every smallest element has a role and follows its appointed figure. Medieval artists were fond of depicting the Dance of Death; but the Dance of Life would be a more accurate concept. From the electrons performing their courtly figures within the atom to the cosmic enchainments of the nebulae, from the ordered rhythms of light and electricity to the free-form manoeuvres of jostling corpuscles, every component of nature takes part. What is the cooling of a planet but a change in tempi? What is music but movement of the air? What is death but the re-alignment, at some invisible ballet-master's cue, of a formation of energies? Movement is a riddle which no human mind has solved. Even Newton, who first grappled with it in the seventeenth century (in his 'calculus' system), only did so by imagining it as minute slices of stillness. Motion remains the primal mystery of the universe, and dance which is its poetry, partakes of its divinity.

It is hardly surprising, then, that dance is the oldest of the arts, the one which binds us most closely to the rest of nature. The stars were wheeling in the sky, birds were dipping and gliding and the vine describing its delicate spiral when man was still an incoherent brute. It is in our blood to move and to be moved by movement. Through participation we enter into the energy-field of life itself, and through empathy we can share its mysteries. Galileo's cry 'It moves!' could be echoed by the response 'It dances!' For dance is structured movement, and structured movement is the basis of all existence.

As humans we can comprehend this, and symbolize it in our dancing. We can even analyse its meaning and purposes. For us today dance has three faces – natural, social and aesthetic.

The three natures of dance not only merge and overlap but actually grow out of each other. The prime element is the simple personal joy of physical movement – the ecstasy of a child running across a field or whirling beside the sea with closed eyes and the sound of the waves as music. Rhythmic movement is a concomitant of life (the heart beats, the lungs swell and shrink, the veins weave their complex choreography through the living tissue) and a natural reaction to emotion, from the ape rocking on his shelf to a human head rolling in extremities of grief or sexual bliss.

The social aspect of dancing also contains elements of psychology. Its function as a cohesive element in a group has been examined by anthropologists and can be felt by anybody joining in a party hop. The subtleties of its language are used even today to distinguish subgroups in a society; it will be 'knees-up!' in the pub and waltzing in the drawing room, just as the peasants were jigging two hundred years ago while their masters trod a minuet. A dance style or even a step is – as choreographers know to their advantage – an immediate clue to class, period, nationality, and character.

Fascination with movement as such has led artists in recent years to experiment with the simulated movement of numerical series or sequences and above all to explore the possibilities of kinetic art, or 'the movement movement', in which the materials actually alter position. In its highest form dance contains not only this element but also the infinitely rich ingredient of the human personality. It is the perfect synthesis of abstract and human, of mind and intellect and emotion, discipline and spontaneity, spirituality and sex-appeal to which dancing aspires; and in dance-as-communication, which is my concern here, it is the most vivid presentation of this act of fusion which represents the ideal performance.

There are many ways of stalking this ideal, as history shows. With slow or sudden shifts in the nature of society or conditions, different emphases are laid on different ingredients. As dancing (like sport) has changed from a participatory to a spectator experience, new expedients have been devised to intensify the communication between performers and audience, ranging from sheer weight of numbers to gymnastic virtuosities, from novel staging to unusual accompaniment. But the basic appeal remains the same – the transmission of a state of awe and excitement (whether exhilarating, emotionally moving or simply aesthetic) from performer to spectator.

The difficulty of defining this experience explains the complexity of the qualities needed to produce it. An audience can be set on fire by spectacle or histrionics, by skill or explosive energy, by graceful lyricism or boisterous comedy. It can be stirred by unusual arrangements of steps or figures, by the physical beauty of the dancers or by dramatic stage devices. It can be stimulated by originality or delighted by the familiar. The effect may be dominated by the choreographer, the designer, the musician or the dancer. In the long run it is the last who counts most. The history of dance is the history of dancers. The actual point of contact between the choreographer and the audience is the performer, in whose body the whole range and history of movement must reverberate. There are as many ways of conveying this hidden message as there are artists: mere skill or grace or speed or beauty is not enough. Rich harmonics are as necessary to a great dancer as to an instrument in an orchestra.

In an art which, until our own day, depended entirely on memory – as poetry did in the time of Homer – even such master-performers were doomed to short, ephemeral fame. But in our own time a vital change has occurred which will surely affect the whole future. We can see the dance of the past only through the work of the artists who recorded it – records in which the conventions of painting played as big a part as the conventions of dancing. The invention of photography has changed all that. Today we can not only see the physical forms of the dancers as they were – in films we can actually watch the tracks and tempi of their movements. The record is still partial – the impact of the human presence can only be guessed at – but it is true within its limits. Equally important is the emergence of systems of dance notation which can preserve the whole structure of a ballet, as a music score freezes a symphony. With these aids, dance history is translated from a hobby into a discipline: it can also be a source of excitement and joy.

Egyptian deity.
Painted pottery, *c.* 4000BC

II On the Banks of the Nile

European culture springs from ancient Greece, and Greek culture was deeply rooted in Egypt; it is on the banks of the Nile that any history of western dance must begin. Prehistoric records of dancing appear in many sites, and there are some especially striking ones in North Africa. A rock-painting shows a man hopping with his leg lifted in exactly the same movement as later appears in Egyptian hieroglyphs, and on a vase from El Amrej, painted around 2500BC, we can see a girl, accompanied by companions with castanets or clappers, dancing with arms over her head in a position used today in classical ballet. Dance may be an ephemeral art, but it is a persistent one.

The gesture with the arms resembles that found in many Cycladic tomb figures, and may be associated with mourning. Certainly the Egyptians, with their vivid sense of the afterlife, attached particular importance to burial rites, and dance played a big part in these ceremonies. First came the mourning ritual, performed mainly by women, some of them probably hired for the occasion. There was doubtless much weeping and wailing while the dancing included stylized gestures imitating scooping up earth and scattering it over the head. Then came the solemn procession to the tomb, in which each stage was strictly laid down by priestly tradition, as the body went through the processes of blessing and embalming and was finally carried to the grave. In this ritual high officials and priests and relatives all played their part, as well as hired artists to perform the 'muu' dances.

Writing to a courtier around 2000BC King Senwosret Kheperkare promised him that, after death, 'You will be placed under a canopy, bulls will draw your hearse, musicians will go before you and a dwarf dance will be performed before the doors of your tomb.' The Egyptians seem to have woven the antics of dwarfs and pygmies into their religious ceremonies, in the same way as grotesque figures were used in the Far East to frighten away evil spirits. 'Hurry home!' wrote a scribe to a traveller in the Sixth Dynasty. 'Bring back with you the pygmy you found in the Land of the Spirits. May he live and be in good health and fresh to dance the sacred dances to cheer the heart of Neperkare, King of Upper and Lower Egypt. When he embarks with you on board ship see that proper men are with him on both sides taking care that he does not fall into the water. See that proper men sleep beside him at night and make inspection ten times. My Lord longs to see the pygmy more than all the presents from Sinai and Punt.'

The King was admittedly only four years old at the time; but pygmies were universally prized, being in short supply. The so-called sacred 'dwarf-dances' seem frequently to have been performed by men of normal size, as can be seen on wall-paintings.

The curious art-conventions of the Egyptians, which demanded that different parts of the body should be drawn from different points of view – arms and legs from the side, body and eyes full-face – do not hinder a vivid impression of these processional dances emerging from their paintings and carvings; they seem to have been performed mainly by women, with weaving movements of the arms over the head and rhythmic shuffling steps. But it is more difficult to get an idea of the next phase of the ceremony, which probably involved more active exercises performed by men, in which scenes of mortal and superhuman contest were solemnly imitated. These half-mimed scenes would eventually lead to the dance-drama of today and were highly developed. One relief clearly shows six such variations for the dancer, each with a (somewhat unintelligible) name – something like: Longing, Emancipation, Stealing Gold, Abduction, Depression, and Plunder. In another scene two girls are miming a victorious King with defeated rival. (This scene was painted on a make-up palette belonging to King Narmer.)

More lively still – and harder for the Egyptian artist to depict – were the general dances which seem to have followed, like the 'wake' in some modern burial customs. These very likely involved the whole congregation and resembled the lively acrobatic entertainment provided at every religious festival.

These feast-days were frequent in the Egyptian calendar. It was customary to celebrate every conceivable phase of the year, as well as personal anniversaries. Folk dancing of the kind usual in the rest of Africa must have marked rustic occasions like the harvest festival in honour of the god Min, when farm hands joined in a stick-dance. A record from the Illahun temple of King Senwosret (1906BC–1887BC) shows that it employed twelve full-time artists – five Asians, two negroes, one Egyptian and four unspecified performers. They were expected to perform at the New Year, the Night Festival of the Floods, the New Moon, the King's Day, Sand Removal Day, the Hitching of Bulls, the festivals of Spokar and Hathor and the beginning of the Five Extra Days (the awkward Egyptian calendar had twelve months of thirty days). The professional dancers – mostly foreigners – led a busy life.

Most of these ceremonies were cheerful ones, especially no doubt those dedicated to Hathor, the goddess of beauty, music and dancing. In the Dendera temple devoted to her a song evidently intended for the performers was recorded: 'We beat the drum of the Spirit, we dance to Her Holiness, we praise Her image to the heavens. She is the Lady of the Sistrum, the Mistress of Jangling Necklaces.' (The sistrum was a musical instrument with magic powers.)

While it is dangerous to generalize from the relatively few surviving images by artists working in media and conventions very unsuited to recording movement, it appears – as might be expected – that dance changed very slowly in Egypt over the centuries. It seems that it became progressively less dignified – but it may be that artistic conventions simply became less strict. The Pharaoh himself took part in sacred rituals – in one example we see him first sitting on a throne, then removing his robe to dance four times round a field in a short kilt. Secular dancing was not considered suitable for the higher classes, but the professional performers evidently developed a sophisticated technique. The general movement was probably sinuous and fluid, with much use of the hands (particularly after the introduction of 'bayadère' dances from India around 1500BC); but even the solemn ritual dances seem to have demanded acrobatics, especially a backward somersault, which is depicted in many scenes from the earliest times; it evidently symbolized the circular rhythms of nature and also perhaps the return of the spirit to the earth at the moment of death.

In later ages such movements became elements in mere entertainment (they

can be seen in the bull-jumping ceremonies in ancient Crete) and were accompanied by the many manoeuvres to be seen on inscriptions – solos, group formation dances, athletic movements in which several performers swing round and round a central figure, and acrobatic pyramids. A young Syracusan wrote from Memphis in the fourth century BC describing an entertainment which had doubtless lasted for centuries:

> Then came forward a group of dancers who jumped about in all directions, gathered together again, climbed on top of each other with incredible dexterity, mounting on shoulders and heads, forming pyramids reaching to the ceiling of the hall, then descended suddenly one after the other to perform new jumps and admirable somersaults. Without stopping, they danced on their hands, paired off, one placed his head between his legs and his partner then lifted him in turn and returned to the original position, each of them alternatively being lifted and, as he fell, lifted his partner up.

In earlier centuries the sexes seem to have been strictly segregated; there are no pictures of boys and girls dancing together. But by the fourth century things had evidently changed:

> At a given sign the centre of the hall was taken by a male and female dancer who were provided with clappers. These were made out of two small pieces of wood round and concave, held in the palms, and gave rhythm to the dancing steps when suddenly knocked together. The two danced separately or together in harmonious configurations mixed with pirouettes, parting and coming together, the young dancer running after the girl and following her with expressions of tender desire, while she kept fleeing from him turning and pirouetting as if refusing his amorous advances.

15

The wooden 'castanets' appear in many dancing scenes, but accompaniment was provided also by musical instruments such as the lyre or harp, flute, lute and tambourine; stamping, singing and clapping were also no doubt normal. In the ritual dances the girls seem to have worn long semi-transparent robes, sometimes held by a thin girdle, though for more active movements they appear to have adopted the short skirt and bare torso which was the ordinary dress for men, or even danced totally naked (as did some of the men); but this effect may be the result of pictorial convention. They were adorned with necklaces, bracelets and ankle ornaments (more simple for the men, who sometimes wore high head-dresses made of plaited reeds). The girls adopted shoulder-length wigs or else an arrangement of three plaits, the thick one at the back ending in a heavy knob designed to make it swing. Sometimes a cake of fat mixed with scent and spices was attached to the top of the head so as to emit sweet smells as it melted and ran down the face. Such exaggerated dressing-up was abandoned in the later New Kingdom years for more lyrical costumes like those worn in Greece, though at religious festivals these were opened down the front in the curious belief that the girls' nakedness would scare off demons.

In secular entertainments the borderline between acrobatics and dancing must have been thin, just as it was between juggling and conjuring. A strong element of mime seems to have played a part in most of the dancing. We know that ritual 'passion-plays' were regularly performed, showing for instance the resurrection myth of Osiris; these certainly included dance-numbers such as imitation combats, as well as mime-scenes. There is a painting in which five girls are shown symbolizing the wind; we can see the fearsome god Bes protecting the Sun from demons by prancing and grimacing; and, if Lucian's account (written long afterwards) is to be believed, some dancers 'translated into expressive movements the most mysterious tenets of their religion, the transformation of gods into animals and above all their love affairs.' All the seeds of modern ballet from fairy tale to erotic duets and abstract ritual were planted in Egypt.

III The Cult of Dionysus

Dance customs, dance formations, even dance steps must have travelled backwards and forwards across the eastern Mediterranean from the earliest times. The island of Crete, the nursery of Greek civilization, lies less than 200 miles off the Egyptian coast and the links between the arts of the Nile and those of the Minoans were close. But there were deep underlying differences between them. While to the Egyptians life after death was vivid and of enormous importance, the Cretans were more interested in life on earth. Their gods were actively involved in daily activities of which survival after death was only a shadowy echo. This change in emphasis is visible in the traces of dance which have survived in Cretan art.

Unquestionably it played a role in the religious festivals of the island, but it seems to have been less solemn and processional than in Egypt. The *geranos* dance which flourished in later years at Delos, the shrine of Apollo, was obviously descended from a Cretan ceremony based on the myth of Theseus and the labyrinth. The dancers held a rope which represented the thread of Ariadne; as the dance-leader unravelled it they followed a complicated figure leading them in a left-hand spiral (symbolizing death) to the centre and then outwards to the right (symbolizing rebirth).

Another dance, perhaps connected with the same myth, involved a priestess dancing with a snake in each hand, probably performing serpentine movements. With the short bolero jacket and the full skirt which was the normal Cretan costume for women, this must have closely resembled the Spanish flamenco dances of today, and may have been an ancestor of them. At the same time the young men doubtless showed their agility in running and jumping movements. Cretan men were so famous for their dancing skill, in fact, that Homer in the *Iliad* made Aeneas say to one of them, Meriones: 'Even though you are a dancer I might have stopped you with my spear.' He wrote nostalgically of 'the dancing floor which once, in spacious Knossos, Daedalus made for Ariadne of the fair locks; there youths and maidens worth many oxen would join hands in the dance.'

The young men's skill culminated in the acrobatics performed around and over the bulls which were the centre of Minoan cult. Here the back-somersault of the Egyptians took on new dancing forms. They may well have been accompanied by rhythmic clapping and chanting from the audience, or congregation, perhaps even by musicians artfully reaching a crescendo at the critical moment, as a modern orchestra follows a virtuoso ballet dancer.

The Minoans were a sybaritic people and the charms of the young were clearly exploited for entertainment as well as for military training and religious ritual. As always, sacred festivals were also the occasion of social and sexual activity. Sappho wrote of 'the Cretan woman dancing in rhythm around the altar with her delicate feet, treading the soft smooth flowers of the meadow', and the emphasis on elaborate make-up and hair-styles, and the exaggerated ornament and body culture of the Cretans, show that to them dancing must have been as much for display as for spiritual uplift.

Even further from the mystic rituals of the Nile were the Spartans, who developed dance as a practical social exercise. From the age of seven Spartan children of both sexes were given exercises to train them in combat-

Opposite: dancing faun. Marble. Roman copy of Greek original on the Borghese vase

Below: dancer and flute player. Greek vase decoration, *c.* 450BC

movement. They developed a marching-dance called the *embaterion* and valued the disciplines of dance so highly that when flattering their statesmen and generals they sometimes gave them the epithet 'dance-leader'. But their most famous war dance was the Pyrrhic Dance, which was made compulsory for all troops, as it was believed (according to Plutarch) to 'inflame courage and give strength to persevere in the path of honour and valour'. Another military dance, the *kurates* (thought to have originated in Crete), was performed at festivals by citizens of high rank; it was a manly affair in which (to quote Lucian) 'sword clashed and shield and inspired heels drummed martial rhythms on the ground'. A delicate version, the 'Memphitic Dance' with lightweight shields, was even devised for women and children. 'Now they turned like a wheel,' wrote Apuleius of one such display. 'Then, holding hands, they formed a long oblique line, then danced toward each other in fours, separated, and crossed in seeming confusion.'

The practice of war-dances as training for soldiers became widespread in Greece. Herodotus, in his *Anabasis*, described a scene during a halt on a long march.

Veiled dancer from Alexandria. Bronze, *c*. 200BC

First some Thracians stood up and began a shield dance to the flute, in which, with great skill, they executed high leaps and swung their spears; then they rushed to each other as though they would attack; but it was all make-believe when one of them sank to the ground. The victor removed his opponent's armour and went off singing while other Thracians carried the loser away as if he were dead; but he was not harmed. Then the Aeneans and Magnetans stood up and danced a shield dance called the *xarpeia*, which went thus: one dancer lays his shield down and sits thoughtfully beside it, looking around as if nervous, then a robber comes and attacks him.

Evidently singing and mime were added to the martial manoeuvres which are depicted in many drawings and carvings.

Dancing of a gentler nature for men was approved by public opinion. Plato regarded it as a help to the attainment of balance and harmony, while Socrates admired it as a way to manliness and control. 'He who honours the gods best in dance will be the best in battle,' he declared, and he was described by Xenophon in middle age asking a Syracusan to give him dancing lessons; when his companions laughed he treated them to a philosophical lecture.

The Spartans seem even to have choreographed their real fighting. 'Music accompanies this people in every movement,' wrote Lucian. 'They advance on the enemy with almost rhythmical step and in the battle itself, after the flute has shrilled the signal to attack, rhythm and melody control the manoeuvres of the soldiers. They have really achieved through this musical discipline a superiority over all others.'

But the purely physical approach to dance turned out (as always) to be only a sideline. It was the mystic element which was to prove the ancestor of its later development, and Dionysus – not Zeus nor even Apollo – who was to be its attendant deity. There was dancing at most festivals in Greece, and

Pyrrhic dance. Relief. Roman copy of Greek original of 400BC

there were mysteries celebrated at many of them, such as the torch-dances connected with the worship of Orpheus; but it was the ritual associated with Dionysus which was to evolve into those performances which led to modern drama, and the areas where they were performed which were to turn into our modern theatre.

The worship of Dionysus was introduced into Greece at a relatively late, post-Homeric period from the north and east. It brought with it the conception of personal union with the god through private ecstasy – in contrast to intercessional magic by priests – and prescribed the use of stimulants such as wine to reach a state of self-abandon. This emotional approach appealed strongly to the downtrodden Greek women, and the prim chain-dances portrayed in early Greek painting soon gave way to scenes in which long-haired Maenads (as the god's followers were called) dressed in long foreign robes whirled and leapt round his altar in ceremonies which seem to have ended in licensed sex activity. According to Diodorus:

> In many towns of Greece, every alternate year, Bacchanalian assemblies of women gather together and it is the custom for maidens to carry the thyrsus [which bore a phallic symbol] and to revel together, honouring and glorifying the god: and for married women to worship the god in organized bands and to revel in every way to celebrate the presence of Dionysus, imitating the Maenads who of old, it is said, constantly attended the god.

The male participants dressed in the shaggy pelts of the goat, which was the 'totem animal' of Dionysus, and took the part of satyrs, whose clumsily amorous movements were to lead in later centuries to comedy and farce.

These celebrations of organized disorder must – like modern pop festivals – have combined individual improvisation with regular dance figures, accompanied by pipes and tambourines and cymbals, and by the sixth century BC they were not only taking place regularly in fixed centres – the Theatre of Dionysus at Athens was the main one – at each of the seven annual festivals of the god, but a firmly structured programme had been established. This was the *dithyramb* (alluding to the mythical double-birth of the god) which consisted of a solemn singing and dancing entrance by the chorus, followed by three or four episodes of Homeric myth chanted by the sacred bard, and ending with a choral exodus.

23

The form of the ritual seems to have changed quite rapidly. It permitted the chorus to consist of satyrs and this led to a division into tragic and comic entertainments. By 500BC Thespis had established regular performances of new plays at the Athens theatre every March festival and himself introduced an 'actor' to make responses to the choral chants. Soon there were three professional actors, backed up by a chorus of amateurs provided by different cities. These numbered fifteen for tragedies (the word 'tragedy' is derived from the Greek for 'goat', the sacred animal of the god) and twenty-four for comedies. They were costumed by the impresario (who was exempted from taxation for his pains) and were specially trained for the occasion in song and dance. They went barefoot and wore no masks, whereas the actors – who had to take many roles as the art of drama developed – wore massive boots and were completely masked. Some of the masks were female, but all the performers, both actors and chorus, were men.

At the start the dramatist was expected to act and sing and dance himself; Aeschylus was his own chorus-leader (or *choryphaios*, a title which has persisted till today in the *coryphées* or leaders of the *corps de ballet*), while Sophocles, who had led a band of dancing youths through the streets of Athens after the victory of Salamis, apparently excelled in his youth in the role of Nausicaa dancing on the beach in a ball-game. The dramatist was also expected to choreograph, and Thespis's pupil Phrynichis boasted that he had invented more dance figures than there are waves in a stormy sea. What exactly these dance figures were we can only guess. We know that the solemn steps which introduced tragedies were called *emmeleia*, while the more acrobatic dances suitable for comedy – often bordering on the obscene – were the *sikinnis* or the even more risky *kordax*.

With the emergence of dramatic poets such as Aeschylus and Sophocles, Euripides and Aristophanes, the role of the song and dance chorus declined into mere musical interludes. Its stately exodus was replaced by Euripides with the trick ending of the *deus-ex-machina* (made possible by the development of the changing-tent or *skena* into a permanent backdrop) and a raised stage to show off the actors cut into the round dancing floor or *orchestra* which had been the performing area (the name survives in the phrase 'orchestra stalls'). The total-theatre concept was fading, leaving the way open for the development of the separate arts – poetry, drama, music and dance.

At the same time the divine character of the performance, in which all the participants became part of the god's holy band, began to disappear. Troupes of mummers were imported from Syracuse, bringing domestic comedies and including the first woman players, and the performers split off into parties of entertainers. By 300BC they had their own union, the Artists of Dionysus Guild, and were touring round the Mediterranean. With them they carried the seeds of the next phase in the story of theatrical dance.

IV Pantomines and Decadence

The shift of power from Greece to Italy in the last centuries before Christ, with Rome replacing Athens as the cultural centre of Europe, marked a vital change in the character of dance. Not only did the Romans of that time have no traditions of dancing, but they had no tradition of the theatre. Their culture was a secular one, with little sense of mystery and religious ritual, and then as now it seems to have been aural rather than visual. Significantly, the name 'theatre' is derived from the Greek verb meaning to see, while 'auditorium' comes from the Latin word for hearing: it could have been foretold that opera would become the national art of Italy.

The Etruscans, who inhabited the region north of Rome, did have a strong dance sense; and as early as 364BC they are recorded by Livy as performing in Rome at a ceremony designed to ward off a plague. Their word for dancer, *ister*, became the Roman term for actor (*histrio*) and so passed into the whole histrionic vocabulary. They favoured acrobatic dances, which they associated with athletics. But it was from the Greek settlements in South Italy and Sicily (particularly Syracuse), and from Greece and its colonies in Syria and Egypt, that theatrical entertainments, and with them dance styles, spread into Rome. These were already different from the native Greek lyrical and tragic performances. The troupes which came from Syracuse were called 'mime' actors, but in fact what they offered were broad burlesque shows in which speaking and singing – and girls – played a big role. These developed into a form which was to prove for some centuries even more popular, the entertainment known as the pantomime.

It is from this theatrical recipe that modern dance-theatre is descended, for (confusingly) it consisted of either a group of dumb-show actors and dancers miming a dramatic story while a chorus chanted the words, or – in its later and more sophisticated form – a single dance-mime who, with the aid of masks, acted out the whole story single-handed, to the accompaniment of music. While lyrical dance is descended from Greek religious celebrations, narrative ballet clearly goes back to Roman pantomime.

During the austere days of the Republic, theatre and dance were frowned on (Cicero remarked that only a drunk man would dance), though Pompilius described an Etruscan troupe at the Roman games in 212BC performing in the city while the Carthaginians were hammering at the gates. But the prosperity which accompanied the first days of the Empire seems to have led to a wave of popularity for the pantomime which, around 22BC became an absolute mania in which the emperor himself was caught up. As was to happen frequently in the future, the prosperity of the art was tied up with the appearance of star performers. These were not Romans; like Russian dancers descending on the West in our own century, two foreign performers arrived in Rome armed with exotic glamour and fitted with the talent to support it. The first was Bathyllos, a native of Alexandria in Egypt, probably Greek in origin. He was young and handsome, with a style which in modern ballet terms would be called *demi-caractère*; he excelled in broad dramatics of the kind known as the *saltatio hilaria* or comic dance: it included plots like Satyr and Amor or Echo and Pan. Bathyllos skilfully played all the roles, but according to Juvenal he was particularly successful in female parts, especially that of Leda. He attracted the admiration of the rich Maecenas (an Etruscan with aesthetic interests) who became his devoted patron. 'He made even the famous mime Thymila look like a peasant,' it was remarked.

His rival was called Pylades. He came from Sicily and was probably also from a Greek family. More serious and dignified than Bathyllos (he wrote a treatise on dancing, which has disappeared), he was what we should now call a *danseur noble*, preferring lofty themes taken from ancient Greek mythology. The rivalry between the two stars became frantic. The most elevated patrician families welcomed them for private entertainment, while their public appearance with their companies – up to sixty performers – excited the crowds to a point where rioting broke out between their fans and Augustus had to suppress the performances. At this time there were already sixty feast days in the year, of which forty included a theatrical entertainment(followed by a circus). Often there were two performances going on simultaneously in the same town. Four centuries later there were 175 holidays, of which one hundred were celebrated with pantomimes.

We know the names of only a few of the dances performed – the *bibasis* in which the performers skipped like antelopes, the *enlaxtismos* which included high kicks, the *thermystris* which demanded beating the feet together; and a dance resembling the movements of a crane.

From both literary and visual sources and by the use of common sense, it can be deduced that in Greek and Roman times dancing was nearer to the style surviving today in the East than to modern European movement. Apart from the flimsy foreign-looking dresses of the followers of Dionysus, the normal costume for both the chorus in a Greek play and for the Roman pantomime soloists was full and heavy (to conceal changes of sex) and elaborately caparisoned. Moreover all the performers wore masks – lighter than the open-mouthed head-dresses worn by the principal actors in a play, but constricting nonetheless. The legs and feet must have been used mainly to mark the rhythm or for striking dramatic poses, while the torso carried the 'melody' by graceful twisting and swirling, and the arms became the most expressive features. The hands were of particular importance. 'You seem to be able to talk with your hands!' exclaimed an admirer to a dancer in Lucian's dialogue (the assumption that speech is superior is typically Roman); there is no mention of feet, and in the fifth century Nonnos wrote in his *Dionysika* of a dancer 'with nods his only words, a hand his mouth, and fingers for a voice.'

There was nothing sacred about this dancing, and the performers were very much part of the general society. They were usually slaves or, at best, 'freedmen'. Some of them were highly respected – Nero's first tutor was a dance teacher – but others clearly traded on their attractions. They took great pains with their appearance (Callenus writes of a depilatory recommended by Paris, of whom the Emperor Lucus Verus was enamoured) and made free of their favours: Trajan had a dancer-companion called Pylades (famous names were passed on from artist to artist), and Commodus favoured one called Septentrio, while Livy reports that no less than two senators died in the embraces of one seductive dancer, Myrmidus.

In the theatre such dancers (girls were not permitted at this time on the pantomime stage though they were widely employed for private entertainment, especially those from Cadiz) justifiably earned a scandalous reputation, which brought reproaches from austere spirits such as Seneca, who complained of the difference between the effeminate dances popular in his time and those of old, when on feast days the citizens 'stamped out a triple rhythm in manly style'. But this did not prevent them taking part in public ceremonies, even at funerals such as that of Vespasian in AD79, when a dancer (according to Suetonius) followed the coffin, miming the character and exploits of the dead emperor. Writers such as Lucan and Statius did not shrink from composing libretti for *fabulae salticae*, and the moralist and historian Plutarch thought fit to remark on the importance, in dancing, of footwork, stage movement and hand gestures.

The craze could obviously lead to exaggeration – in Nero's time the eighty-year-old Aelia Catella was seen dancing in the Youth Games; to absurdity – Nero himself is described as performing the role of Vergil's Dido, possibly in the Dionysus Theatre in Athens which had been remodelled for his performance; and to licence – Messalina indulged (according to Tacitus) in orgiastic Maenad dances and had an affair with a performer, whom her husband put to death. But in a more moderate and civilized form dance became, for the first time, part of the education of well-brought-up citizens. 'I let myself be taken to a dancing class', said Scipio disapprovingly in the second century (according to Macrobius), 'and there, by God, I saw over fifty girls and boys, including a youth of less than twelve years old . . . the son of a public servant, who was performing with clappers a dance of which any wretched slave would be ashamed.'

But inexorably the charm of innocent social dance won its way into Roman hearts. In his story of 'Daphnis and Chloe', written about a century later, Longus describes with obvious delight how the aged Dryas danced a gentle version of a Dionysiac dance, the *epilemion*, celebrating the wine harvest, and so pleased the young lovers that they laughingly danced the whole tale of Pan wooing Syrinx. And one of the most eloquent defences of dance ever written came in a dialogue usually ascribed to Lucian, a Syrian who had lived in Athens and died in Egypt in AD190. He describes the young Lykinos trying to convince a sceptical friend that it is not an ignoble art, and – after citing examples from Homer and Sparta and quoting a memorial erected by the Thessalonians 'in honour of Eilaton for having danced well in battle' – he proceeded not only to enumerate the qualities necessary for a great dancer, which included temperament and intelligence as well as skill and a good figure, but to praise dance in elevated terms:

Masked pantomime performer. Wall painting, Herculaneum, *c.* AD50

> With the creation of the universe the dance too came into being, which signifies union with the elements. The round dance of the stars, the figure of the planets among the fixed stars, the beautiful order and harmony in all its movements, is a mirror of the original dance of creation. The dance is the richest gift of the muses to man. By its divine origin it is part of the mysteries and is beloved of the gods and carried out by men into their honour.

Dance had moved a long way from the rugged *bellicipea* war-mimes of

Romulus and the Salian priests, which had a real relationship to fighting (as Byron was to complain centuries later: 'You have your Pyrrhic dance as yet, where is the Pyrrhic phalanx gone?') and perhaps even further from the inspired Dionysian revels in which both participants and spectators partook of divinity. It had turned into a social pastime and a highly commercialized public entertainment ranging from the obscene to the respectable. Apuleius described a stage performance in Corinth in the second century. In front of a painted movable scene representing Mount Ida a company represented the story of the Judgement of Paris. It might have been the model of an eighteenth century ballet at Versailles.

In an alarmingly short time the healthy art of 'pantomime', or what we should call dramatic dance solos, began to degenerate. Already by the death of Vespasian in AD79 a dog had taken the principal role and the introduction of women on the stage (by the fourth century it was reckoned that there were 3000 of them in Rome alone) encouraged a tendency towards a music-hall type of entertainment such as the water-ballet described by Martial in which half-naked girls performed acrobatics. Sometimes the dancers must have been mere children. A tombstone of about AD100, still standing in the south of France, bears the touching Latin inscription: 'To the memory of the boy Septentrio, aged twelve, who danced twice at Antibes and gave pleasure.' Tiberius took the drastic step of banishing all performers, but they soon returned and a hundred years later, around AD180 we find Marcus Aurelius merely attempting to reduce their exorbitant fees. Scipio shut the dancing schools which had shocked him so, and slowly the art of 'pantomime' died out, to be replaced by the burlesque acting shows, or mummers, which had preceded it and by the crude attractions of the circus. Dance theatre was already dead in Rome when in AD410 Rome itself was destroyed.

Funeral dance. Fresco from a tomb at Ruvo, *c.* 450BC

V Medieval Revels

'Le Bal des Ardents', Paris, 1393. During the festivities, the French king, Charles VI, disguised as a Savage, was nearly burnt to death. From a medieval illustration

The fall of the Roman Empire marked a total change in all the arts of Europe. Its prosperity had fostered a hedonistic culture in which life was decidedly agreeable for a fairly large section of society. Entertainment, both in private and public, was enjoyed and approved by most people, from poets like Ovid and Horace, to the swarming crowds of citizens and slaves.

A few voices, however, were consistently raised against it. Both Seneca and Cicero had spoken out in opposition. But its severest critics were the elders of the new Christian sect who deplored the threat to morality presented by actors and dancers. In the third century Tertullian, in his *De Spectaculus*, was pronouncing fiercely against them, and the theatre (which with its association with the brutalities of the circus, had certainly reached a low standard at this time) was a fixed target for pious fulminations.

As poverty and brutality spread across Europe in the wake of the invaders from the north, such expensive pleasures died out of their own accord, and the Christian doctrine which set out to alleviate material misery by promises of bliss after death became the refuge of the whole population. Ironically a small relic of the ancient Dionysiac mysteries survived within the Church itself. Dance had played a part in the ritual of several of the small mystic sects in Rome (a dance-chant from a service to Lares and Mars has come down to us: 'Help us, O Lares! Mars, let us not die! Tread the step of the altar, seize the scourge. Summon the Semonians in their round dance. Help us, O Mars!) and dancing persisted in some Christian church services. In the third century St Gregory Thurmaturgos was conducting dance movements in the choir of a

Dancing juggler. Relief, French School, 12th century

church and John Chrysostom, though he disapproved of mime players, is said to have actually danced himself in a ceremony. The symbolic choreography of sacred procession and ritual came close to more active manoeuvres and until recently included actual dancing in some churches in Italy and Spain, for instance the *Los Seises* dances of the choristers in Sevilla (when the Archbishop tried to suppress them, the choir-master took the whole performance to Rome to convince the Pope of their excellence). Indeed there are records of secular performers trying to join in – some masked dancers attempted to invade a church in Paris in 1445 though the atmosphere must have been extremely decorous: there is no trace of dance rhythms in sacred music of the period.

However the general Christian attitude to dance was (and remained for centuries) one of total disapproval. 'It is better to plough or dig ditches on a Sunday than to dance a roundelay', declared St Augustine in the fifth century. It is easy to understand his hostility. Dancing survived at this time mainly in popular festivals at which the peasants tried to forget the hardships of their daily life with revels fortified by beer or wine. Fertility rites from earlier ages were continued in modified form such as the maypole dance, and magic capering reminiscent of the Egyptian pigmy dance or the Satyr dances of the Greeks kept their hold on superstitious and ignorant villagers. Bruegel drew a procession of epileptics undergoing some kind of attempted dancing cure as late as the sixteenth century.

When the dreaded 'millennium' year of AD1000 came and went without incident, the hold of the church slackened and the gentle code of chivalry

Dancer and musicians. Drawing, British, *c*. 1200

penetrated the ruling classes. Even the holiday celebrations included comparatively sophisticated entertainment. The *Roman de la Rose* of the thirteenth century describes boys and girls dancing duets (without touching, of course) and following complicated patterns while the festivals themselves sometimes included a 'jaculator', or *Spielmann*, as he was called in Germany, who – like the pantomime performers of Rome – led the activities, and himself mimed scenes from ancient classical myths and allegories. His role was carried on by the 'troubadours' (who originated in the former Roman district of Provence) whose teams of singers and dancers spread organized entertainment across the whole of Europe. It became usual to keep some such performer in the household; he often became a sort of social tutor, who taught manners to the young and even accompanied them when they left home. In other cases his skills passed to the 'jester' who was expected to be able to dance and sing in his role of family entertainer.

The rustic revels of the village slowly penetrated the precincts of the castle, to become the basis of a new style of dancing. The celebrations which followed the fierce martial competitions known as 'pageants' became so elaborate that they had to be postponed until the evening, when they took place indoors. Here the herald who had controlled the pageantry became a master of ceremonies; singing and acting took place in the great hall and specially composed entertainments known in England as 'disguisements' or later 'masques' (both names arising from the masks worn by the performers) beguiled the nobility.

In 1377 Charles V of France entertained Charles IV of Germany with a display which included two set-pieces, one representing Jerusalem, defended by a band of Saracens and the other a party of Christian knights. The ensuing entertainment involved, not unnaturally, mock battle-dances between the two sides, in which the nobility finally joined.

One entertainment of the time became famous by accident. On 29 January, 1393, the twenty-four-year-old Charles VI of France invited his friends to the wedding of one of the queen's ladies-in-waiting. A certain Hugonin de Guisay was entrusted with the arrangements, which included the usual formal dances, followed by a banquet. Towards midnight the climax was reached – a masquerade of satyrs. Unknown to the audience these consisted of the king himself and five of his courtiers, concealed within shaggy costumes made of linen and flax, with masks over their faces.

For safety's sake strict orders had been given that the 'varlets' holding the torches should stand against the walls. Froissart wrote:

> Soon after, the Duke of Orleans entered into the hall, accompanied by four knights and six torches, and knew nothing of the king's commandment for the torches nor of the mummery that was coming thither, but thought to behold the dancing and began himself to dance. Therewith the king with the five other came in; they were so disguised in flax that no man knew them; five of them were fastened to another; the king was loose and went before and led the device.
>
> When they entered into the hall, every man took so great heed to them that they forgot the torches. The king departed from his company and

went to the ladies to sport with them, as youth required. . . . In this mean season great mischief fell on the other, and by reason of the duke of Orleans. . . . He was so desirous to know what personages the five were that danced, he put one of the torches that his servants held so near that the heat of the fire entered the flax (wherein if fire take there is no remedy) and suddenly was a bright flame and so each of them set fire on other. The pitch was so fastened to the linen cloth and their shirts so dry and fine and so joining to their flesh that they began to bren and cry for help.

Court dance, from *De Practica seu Tripudii*, a treatise on dancing by Guglielmo Ebreo, 1463

All but one (who ran to a water butt in the buttery) were fatally burned.

An amateur attempt to provide professional entertainment had ended (not for the last time) in disaster – it came to be known as 'Le Bal des Ardents', – but it had marked an important step in the evolution of dance. It started the breakdown of the rigid barrier between the sexes which had been maintained since the earliest times (it is ironic that this puritanical custom which had been observed pretty strictly through centuries of pagan culture should finally lapse in the heyday of the Church): the performers were still male, but they were permitted, even expected, to 'sport with the ladies'. An equally important change was the participation of the highest society in the dancing, not in a solemn ritual but from sheer enthusiasm.

At the wedding of Prince Arthur and Catherine of Aragon in 1490 in Westminster Hall a courtly entertainment was provided. A waggon decorated to represent a castle was drawn in by 'four great bestes with cheynys of gold', each composed of two men; looking out of the windows were eight 'goddly and fresshe ladies'. This was followed by a 'ship' bearing two ambassadors from the 'Mownte of Love' who laid siege to the castle. They had no success until a third waggon representing a hill was drawn in; from this descended a bevy of knights who forced the ladies to yield. General rejoicing, led by Prince Arthur, concluded this happy conquest, in which the knights 'daunced togyders dyvers and many goodly daunces'. The floor was then cleared, and the whole company joined in the revels, with such abandon that the future Henry VIII 'sodenly cast off his gowne and dauncyd in his jaket.'

This democratic mixing of entertainers and entertained seems to have started cautiously. By the end of the fourteenth century both had begun to take part in the final revels, but in separate groups. A hundred years later they were mingling freely, with the mummers and dancers partnering the ladies of the castle. We are only a step from the court diversions which were to lead directly to classical ballet.

VI Entrées and Entremêts

Something provincial characterized even the most ambitious entertainments of the Middle Ages, with their jousting and tournaments, their buffoons and home-made pageantry; and their dancing remained unpretentious. Sophisticated balls such as those given by the dukes of Burgundy would consist of a sedate parade in steady rhythm using steps of the kind known as the *basse danse*, followed by a lively skipping measure based on country dancing. Such feudal revels were already on their way out by the end of the fifteenth century; a whole new culture was spreading across Europe from Italy. In 1393 the King of France had nearly been burned to death dressed up as a shaggy monster: a hundred years later, in 1490, Leonardo da Vinci was designing an extravaganza to entertain the Duke of Milan, built round a learned theme based on astronomy. The Renaissance had taken place.

The Duke's diversion was by no means the first of its kind. Only the year before he had been entertained (in Tortona) at a banquet in which each dish was accompanied by a suitable dance diversion. They were ingeniously worked into the story of Jason and the Argonauts. The Golden Fleece suggested roast lamb, Actaeon ushered in the boar and venison, nymphs carried on poultry and peacocks, Neptune and the River gods supplied the fish, and the whole meal was washed down with Hebe's nectar. The entries of the different dance groups, as well as the variations during the intermissions between the courses, passed into the language of dancing and cookery as *entrées* and *entremêts*.

Such elaborate diversions (the Brunelleschi brothers had developed the visual ingredients at the start of the century) were not unusual at this period, but the wealth of the new patrons and the talent of the artists involved produced an explosion of showmanship in which science and architecture, music and mechanics, learning and imagination joined with dance and the theatrical arts to produce the composite art form which was to develop rapidly into classical ballet.

Leonardo's entertainment was typical of its kind. It opened with a general dance led by the Duke and Duchess, which was followed by short variations in various national styles, starting with a Spanish number (the Duke had chosen a Spanish costume for himself, in mulberry coloured velvet with a cloak of black velvet lined with brocade of gold on a white ground – perhaps designed by Leonardo). French, German and Polish numbers came next, with a parade of Turks. Then came 'Il Paradiso', with revolving planets and poets chanting the praises of the Duchess, while lights shining through coloured glass twinkled like stars. It was a classic gala performance.

The passion for order and proportion which pervaded the new culture as an echo of Greek and Roman thinking quickly penetrated the world of dance. As early as 1416 an Italian called Domenico di Piacenza had written a treatise on dancing in which he laid down the qualities necessary to a performer – musicality, style, a feeling for space, elevation and mood – and then analysed the components of various dances. He divided them into twelve movements, nine natural and three artificial and named four species in accelerating tempi – the stately *Basse danse*, the *Quadrilena*, the *Saltarello* (faster, with hops and beats) and the vigorous bagpipe-dance or *Piva*. The

A trick costume for a ballet for the French court, possibly by Jean Bérain. The dancer carries a doll on his back, while his own head seems to be surmounted by a mask. Drawing, late 17th century

Above: grotesque episode in the Fuerst-
enbacher Ritterspiel. Celebrations in
honour of Duke Johann Friedrich von
Württemberg in Stuttgart, 1616. Engravings by Matthäus Merian

Opposite: processional float symbolizing Modesty. Illustration to a manu-
script of Petrarch's *I Trionfi, c.* 1475

Basse danse was the basis of many variations known as *Balli*, which
introduced changing rhythms and sometimes an element of character, such
as a flighty lady wooed by a stranger (this one was called *La Mercantina*).

When it took place in private, the dancing was normally performed by
couples – first the most distinguished pair and then several together. The
music consisted of well-known melodies or at least rhythms (usually in duple
time for the *Basse danse*, though later a triple rhythm was to become popular,
and common time for the quick *Saltarello* or *Piva* which followed). The
development of music as an independent art led to more strictly formalized
patterns: the standard *Basse danse*, for example, became the *Branle*, *Reprise*,
Seconde Reprise and *Tordion*.

Long wide-sleeved gowns must have limited the ladies to the most simple
footwork; as usual in those days, all the emphasis was on the arms and
shoulders and the head – particularly the last, for the ladies wore high and
often elaborate headdresses and coiffures, such as the 'butterfly' in which
diaphanous veils trailed from a wire cage. The men too, were handicapped in
their movements, being hampered by the long pointed indoor shoes
(originally a Polish fancy) which remained in fashion right through the
fourteenth century. They were so popular in England that Edward III
introduced a law that 'no knight under the estate of a lord, esquire or
gentleman, nor any other person, shall wear any shoes or boots having spikes
or points which exceed the length of two inches, under the forfeiture of forty
pence'. This was a heavy penalty at that time for a peccadillo which must have
been a serious obstacle to agility. The men kept their hats on while dancing,
and these were sometimes quite bulky.

The Italian nobility who took part in Leonardo's festivities in Milan were

Design for 'Birds Episode' in 'Il Carnevale Languente' (The Languid Carnival) at the Turin Theatre, choreographed by Filippo d'Aglié for the Duchess of Savoy, sister of Louis XIII, 1647

already wearing more practical clothes – doublets and hose for the men, with manageable shoes, and neat hair styles (buns and curls), for the ladies. Such fashions must have made it possible for the guests to join the professional performers for the final dance – for though carefully arranged and rehearsed, the choreography was still based firmly on the social dances familiar to all the aristocracy.

But the gap between the performers and the audience was opening up fast, encouraged by the popularity of the entertainment offered by strolling open-air players. In northern Europe this took the form mainly of miracle plays (the old Sicilian 'mime' with a religious twist) while in the south it was strongly influenced by the shows commemorating the expulsion of the Moors from Spain, known as Morescas. These two traditions combined in Italy in mixed entertainments which included a large measure of dance and music which was easily absorbed into the imposing processional *trionfo* which rulers like Lorenzo the Magnificent of Florence developed as a symbol of power and commercial dynamism.

The conception of dance as a spectacle, which had been introduced by the Romans, was carried to new heights by their descendants. The simple diversion on the city square or the after-dinner frolics in which the guests could join were becoming splendid and complicated spectacles. The costumes and visual devices created a sharp division between entertainers and entertained; professional tumblers and dancers began to join the courtiers who played the principal roles (including the female parts). The banqueting hall was turning into a private theatre and the audience was inexorably moving towards the passive role it was to play for the next five hundred years.

Another important change had come over the performances. The mimes, actors and dancers who had provided the entertainments in nordic feudal diversions had almost invariably been asked to represent abstract symbols such as Chastity, Hope, Envy or Good Fortune (the travelling miracle plays which had developed, under the influence of the Church, from old mime shows from Sicily, introduced the same device with Christian symbols). In Italy the new entertainments based on classical myths provided vitally new characters – individual heroes and heroines. Allegories persisted – Death, for instance was to remain a familiar character in ballet almost up to today, in various guises – but the impersonation of great personalities, however mythical, opened up a whole new range for the performers. The star-dancer – already a familiar figure in Roman times with his musical back-up group – was standing in the wings ready to reappear with a whole panoply of designers, musicians and artists as support.

Above: Scaramouche, a character in the Commedia dell' Arte. Engraving by Jacques Callot, *c.* 1620

Opposite: costume design by Bernardo Buontalenti, probably for a Florentine Intermezzo, 1589

VII The Courtly Dance

Dance entertainments were to pass through one more stage before they acquired the structure with which we are familiar today, and this entailed a change of scene, from Italy to France. The newly centralized regime in Paris (Louis XI had finally broken his main rival, the Duke of Burgundy, in 1477) was establishing itself as a European power-centre, and this involved demonstrations of conspicuous magnificence. Italian styles in entertainment had begun to seep northwards in the early part of the fifteenth century, with sophisticated and elaborate masquerades based on classical mythology replacing the traditional *basse danses* and tumblers. The new fashion became completely entrenched with the arrival at the Paris court of an Italian princess with a dominating personality, an active mind and a lively interest in the arts. In 1533 the fourteen-year-old Catherine de Medici arrived from Florence to marry Henri II of France; she was to be the most powerful figure in France for the next fifty years.

How vital this time was to be for the history of dance can be gauged from its vocabulary. 'Ballet' – the name used now to describe theatrical dancing – is Italian in origin (from 'ballare', to dance) but it is the French form that has passed into universal currency, and all the technical terms of dancing (unlike those of its related art, music) are French. In the historical relay-race which makes up the story of ballet, France ran a crucial lap.

As in all the arts of that period, activity centred entirely round the ruling establishment. Art was used as a manifestation of majesty, and every branch was called upon to contribute. The result was a mixed-media formula in which poetry, drama, painting, music and dancing played equal roles – with the extra consideration that the dancers could personally illustrate the pyramid of power. Poets and musicians might be professionals, but the main characters of the dance episodes were acted by the court itself, in its varying degrees. From the apex of the ruler himself, the star roles were performed by the highest figures in the land, assisted by every device which could add to their splendour and a full supporting cast. This was the *ballet de cour* or court dance, performed by the nobility for the nobility. It demanded the highest talents in every field, and set not only the style but the standards for future ballets; and it established firmly the structure of stars, coryphées and corps de ballet which reflected the hierarchy of the court and which was to persist to this day.

The first French entertainment of this kind of which we have details (fortunately it became fashionable to print souvenir catalogues complete with scores, libretti and illustrations) was the *Balet des Polonais* given by Catherine in the Tuileries palace in 1573 to celebrate the election of one of her sons as king of Poland. She had already organized some notable festivities, one in 1558, for example, when her eldest son married Mary Queen of Scots, and another rather ominous one, *La Défense du Paradis,* in 1571 in which the theme was the struggle between the Protestants and the Catholics (the notorious massacre of St Bartholomew took place the following year). The 'Polish' ball was quite a modest affair, lasting no more than an hour, and included a generous measure of poetry (eight-nine Latin verses translated by Ronsard, 'well sung though ill composed') besides an allegorical display which incorporated Silenus with four satyrs, and sixteen ladies-in-waiting,

Above: costume representing Music, for the ballet 'Fêtes de Bacchus', performed at the Palais Royal, 1651. Drawing

Below: costumes for Night, in 'La Douairère de Billebahout' ('The Dowager of Bilbao'), 1626. Louis XIII performed as a Persian

each of whom represented a French province. These ladies executed complicated geometrical figures (a French speciality) 'of bizarre intention' to an orchestra of thirty viols.

The simple numbers were a striking success. 'Not one lady failed to memorise their order, all participants having solid judgement and excellent memories.' The real credit must have belonged to their coach, an Italian called Balthasar de Beaujoyeulx (Belgiojoso), and eight years later he was commissioned to devise a far more ambitious production, the *Balet Comique de la Royne Louise*. This event was fully documented and was clearly a superb example of the kind of performance which was the direct ancestor of classical ballet.

It took place in the huge Salle Bourbon of the old Louvre Palace in Paris in 1581 to celebrate the marriage of Queen Louise's sister to Catherine's brother-in-law, and was planned on an ambitious scale. Joy and allegory abounded. The new husband was called the Duc de Joyeuse, the dance director was again Beaujoyeulx; a plaque engraved with a dolphin ('dauphin', also signifying son and heir) was presented to the childless king and queen, and the plot – the rescue of Ulysses from the wicked enchantress Circe – provided for a number of flattering political allusions.

The king sat at one end of the hall, with hundreds of courtiers banked up round three sides of it. The other end was designed as Circe's palace and garden, with glimpses of a town behind. To one side of the hall was a little rustic pavilion representing Pan's grotto; opposite it was the orchestra. Beaujoyeulx had worked out a complete consecutive libretto in which music, poetry, acting and dancing were cunningly combined. After the escaped Ulysses had declared the wrongdoings of Circe and begged the king to help her victims, there was a sung interlude by tritons and sirens, then an entrée for the queen in a magnificent chariot, representing a four-tier fountain, with a dozen duchesses representing naiads. Circe herself appeared with a rather plaintive number – a song entitled 'the complaint of Circe having lost a gentleman'. Glaucus and Thetis sang a duet while the Naiads were joined by eight satyrs for a chorus. A forest-on-wheels bore in Virgins and Dryads: Mercury descended from a cloud and delivered a speech but was lured into Circe's garden, while men whom she had transformed into a stag, a dog, an elephant and a lion ended the act with a grotesque number.

The second act included singing satyrs and dancing nymphs besides more gods and goddesses including the four virtues and Athene, each making his entry on a decorated float. Finally Circe collapsed, struck down by a thunderbolt from Jupiter, who descended from a cloud. De Beaujoyeulx wrote in his memoirs:

It was then that the viols changed key and began to play the entrée of the Grand Ballet, composed of fifteen passages so devised that at the end of each one all turned their heads towards the King. Having arrived before his Majesty, they danced the Grand Ballet of forty passages of geometric figures, some diametrically, some in square, some in a circle, in many and various fashions, and also in a triangle accompanied by a few little squares, and other figures. . . . These geometrical evolutions sometimes took the

form of a triangle with the queen at the top of it; they revolved in a circle, interwove in a chain and traced various figures with a cohesion and accuracy which astonished those present.'

'Entrance of the Great Khan and his followers' in 'La Douairière de Billebahout', 1626. Design by Daniel Rabel

The wedding party, which had started at ten in the evening, ended with a general dance which finished at four the following morning, though pauses for refreshments and royal ceremonies and junketings had probably occupied about half the time. It had been as least as near to opera as to ballet (the word 'comique' denoted simply 'dramatic') but its structure – a unifying theme on which appropriate numbers were hung – was to provide the model for dance entertainments for later generations.

The fashion for court entertainments in the French style soon spread across Europe. In England Queen Elizabeth – herself a passionate dancer – was a frequent patron of the 'masque', a development of the old pageants and 'disguisements' which (with the cooperation of poets like Ben Jonson) gave more prominence to words than to scenic effects or dancing. In Italy – particularly in Turin, where a Francophile citizen composed over forty ballets, and in Parma – elaborate entertainments were popular, though they often contained more singing than dancing. In Florence the wedding of one of Catherine de'Medici's granddaughters was celebrated with a huge show calling on no less than five composers and two librettists, with the painter

Above: 'Bal à la Française; the Stras-
bourg Minuet'. French engraving, 17th
century

Opposite: the 15-year-old Louis XIV as
the Sun King in 'Le Ballet de la Nuit',
1653, the role which gave him his nickname, Le Roi Soleil. Drawing

Bronzino as one of the designers. In Mantua Monteverdi composed *Il Ballo dell' Ingrate* for the Duke.

A curious variety of these spectacles – clearly a descendant of the old tournament – was the equestrian ballet, in which semi-military manoeuvres in geometric style (Beaujoyeulx had defined ballet as 'a geometrical arrangement of several persons dancing together to the diverse harmonies of numerous instruments') were performed by horsemen. These became enormously popular (Monteverdi composed one called *Mercury and Mars*) and took on some unusual forms: in 1608 the *Tournament of the Winds*, performed in Tuscany, called for 120 horsemen taking the part of nymphs. A French libretto later in the century specified 20,000 horses.

Meanwhile a vital development in the history of dance was taking place in Italy. This was the establishment of the permanent proscenium-theatre in place of the temporary stage built at one end of a convenient large hall. The first seems to have been built around 1580. To begin with they provided wide ramps down which the aristocratic performers could move to join their friends in the auditorium; but the gap between players and audience was intensified. This was further widened by the increasing ambitions of the entertainments which demanded expert manoeuvring (involving lengthy rehearsals) and skilled execution of some parts so difficult that only a professional dancer could manage them. As early as 1626 Louis XIII was happily appearing in a ballet called *La Douairière de Billebahaut* alongside not only his handsome friend the Duc de Luynes but also professionals called Marais and Morel, and six years later he was taking the part (as the heroine) in his own ballet *La Merlaison* while Marais exercised his brilliance and speed in the role of a bird.

The character of the show was moving – in France at any rate – towards a predominantly dancing spectacle. The old dramatic genre – the *ballet comique* – had briefly yielded to the sung spectacle or *ballet mélodramatique* which was to develop in Italy into opera; but finally the more lively *ballet à entrée*, which consisted of production numbers with dance interludes, became the greatest favourite. It was that which was to lead in the next century to the narrative ballets still surviving today.

VIII France seizes the Torch

Top: Momus, a character in the 'Bal de St Cloud', 1752. Chalk drawing by Gabriel de St Aubin

Above: Mademoiselle le Fèvre ainée, a dancer in Paris. Drawing, *c.* 1760

With well equipped permanent stages springing up all over Europe, and dance techniques becoming more and more polished (especially in Italy, where the subject had inspired several analytical treatises), and with royal formalities becoming sufficiently flexible to allow highly trained professional performers to participate, the way was open for the launching of dance-theatre as a full-blown art form. The moment had arrived, and the person appeared prompt on cue – Louis XIV of France.

Louis had two passions – himself and the theatre – and he combined them in a phenomenon which was perfectly attuned to his time. At the age of seven he had been entranced by the gambolling monkeys and Indians in an opera put on by his Italian-born guardian Mazarin; and at thirteen he was himself dancing before the court. Two years later, in 1653, he appeared as the star of a sumptuous entertainment titled the *Ballet de la Nuit*, dressed as the sun round which the whole civilized world revolved – hence his nickname, the Sun King.

This kind of symbolism was in line with the allegorical approach usual in such productions, while the figures of the dance, doubtless stately and strictly geometrical in style, reflected the spirit of the Age of Reason. It was an age in which Corneille had written the libretto for a ballet (*Le Château de Bicêtre*), Descartes had – anonymously – done the same for Queen Christina of Sweden, and Molière, some of whose plays, such as *Les Fâcheux*, included dancing and who wrote a *divertissement royal* for one of Louis' last appearances in 1671, did not hesitate to perform character parts alongside professional dancers.

Though the men's costumes were now well fitted for nimbleness, the high-heeled shoes worn by the aristocracy severely limited the possibilities, and decorum prohibited anything more daring than modified ballroom steps like the gavotte, the pavane, the courante or the minuet. These were becoming more and more refined, with dancing-masters training the young in the niceties of properly turned-out legs and elegant, harmonious movements of the arms and head. These gestures, which had already been classified as 'correct' fifty years earlier – arms held wide (to avoid brushing the full skirts worn by both sexes) and feet elegantly pointed to show off buckles and ribbons – became the foundation of the classical ballet idiom, and have since proved capable of many subtle variations.

In his youth Louis must have had some dancing talent, at any rate he appeared in some twenty-seven ballets. He engaged Giovanni Battista Lulli, a Florentine musician and dancer, to compose and supervise his productions and occasionally perform in them (he was a gifted comedian), with important results for both ballet and opera. Pierre Beauchamps was his ballet master. He is credited with the establishment of classical ballet's basic 'five positions', and he stressed technical steps and movements as opposed to the simple geometrical movements then in fashion. In addition the whole spectacle was usually designed by Jean Bérain, whose opulent and ingenious in-terpretations of Greek and Roman costume and magnificent architectural settings created new standards of production; indeed they were reflected in the whole tone of Louis' court at Versailles, which often resembled a majestic stage spectacle. The convention of sumptuously extravagant costumes and high feathered head-dresses was to persist in the French theatre down to our own times, and is still distantly echoed in every Folies Bergère revue.

Louis was positively addicted to dancing. He organized huge entertainments, sometimes lasting all night, at whichever of his several palaces he might be, and he even appeared before the general public (in a work with the daunting title *La Prosperité des Armes de France*); but at thirty he was already becoming fat and somewhat pompous, and he abandoned the dancing floor, though, like other stars, he could be tempted out of retirement on occasion. In 1665, at the age of forty-seven he was taking the role of a nymph in a ballet called *L' Eclogue de Versailles*.

France had now indisputably seized the dance-torch from Italy and its supremacy was sealed in 1661 when Louis – tired of dancing himself – laid the foundation of dance as an independent public art by setting up the Académie Royale de la Danse. It turned out to be an ephemeral foundation, but its function was resumed eight years later by the Académie Royale de la Musique, soon taken over by Lully (now so spelt). This was to prove a lasting organization, eventually to be the Paris Opéra; and in it both women and men were trained for the stage. The court monopoly of dance entertainments was over for ever.

The change was gradual at first. Professionals (accepted for many years in Italy) were allowed at the French court in 1630, and after 1659 convention permitted the highest nobility to appear side by side with those professional performers whose reputation was so murky that the church would not marry or even bury them. In 1672 Lully put on a ballet at his Opéra called *La Fête de l'Amour et de Bacchus* and it was performed by four male professionals and four noblemen, one of whom was the commander-in-chief of an English force loaned to France by Charles II – none other than Charles's own illegitimate son, the Duke of Monmouth. He was to appear in England in the Lully-Molière *Psyche* three years later, perhaps the only British royalty to dance on the London stage (though the sober William of Orange appeared in his youth in Holland).

From now on the history of theatrical dance, or 'ballet' as it was to be universally called, was to be bound up with its creators and interpreters rather than with its noble patrons. Dancers like Jean Balon, choreographers and designers moved into the limelight.

Jean-Baptiste Lully had already made a vital contribution to ballet history under Louis XIV. Shrewd, talented and ambitious he arrived in Paris from Florence as a fourteen-year-old page, adopted the profession of dancer and musician and quickly charmed his way into the king's confidence. As the latter's master-of-music he not only supervised the establishment of the Académie Royale with its dancing annex but developed a new style of dance entertainment, the light comedy-ballet in which music and dance joined with verbal and visual wit to produce a diversion with a unified style. As an ex-dancer he understood the possibilities of the art and he moved it away from pompous spectacle and meaningless diversions towards a popular and coherent form which went back to the performances of the *Commedia dell' arte*. He ventured that the pieces which he produced with the collaboration of Molière, such as *Les Fâcheux* and *Le Bourgeois Gentilhomme* (both are usually presented now as straight dramas) would be 'new to our stage but

Two dancers at the Paris Opéra: Mademoiselle des Chars and, below, Jean Ballon, a famous virtuoso. Engraving after a drawing by Nicholas Bonnart, *c.* 1700

Caricature of the famous dancer from
the Paris Opéra, Auguste Vestris. Wash
drawing by George Dance, 1781

might find authority in antiquity'.

But even more important for the future of ballet was the contribution of a
young French dancer who was to become a great performer, Jean Georges
Noverre. Noverre was born in Paris in 1727 and, after a spell in Potsdam
under Frederick the Great and in the French provinces he was made ballet-
master at the Opéra Comique in Paris. Here, in 1754 he mounted a spectacle
called *Ballet Chinois* in which 'thirty-two vases rose up and hid thirty-two
dancers so that the stage seemed transformed into a Chinese cabinet'.
(Chinoiserie was all the rage at the time and the ballet was a huge success.)
Next year he was invited to London by Garrick and watched him act and
mime before moving to Lyons, where he sat down to write a treatise called
Lettres sur la Danse. They were published in 1760 in Stuttgart where he had
been invited by the Duke of Württemberg, and became a key document in the

story of ballet. In place of the loosely organized patchworks which were the normal entertainments of the time, he proposed a logical extension of Lully's ideas – consistent and serious dance dramas free from intrusive virtuoso interruptions, with choreography based on character and situation rather than personal display, and a clear, close relationship between movement and music, action and design. To this logical structure each element would contribute, with the choreographer as the ultimate controller.

Noverre was particularly dissatisfied with the way dancers were dressed. 'I would have no more of those stiff, cumbersome breeches,' he wrote. 'I would cut down by three-quarters the ridiculous panniers of our ballerinas.' And in addition he put forward a revolutionary idea – that dancers should throw away their masks, 'those hideous faces which conceal nature and show us instead a misshapen and grimacing copy'. The retention of these masks in ballet is one of the most curious phenomena of dance history. They had originated in the religious theatre rituals of ancient Greece; they had been perpetuated in the Roman 'pantomimes', where a single performer would impersonate all the characters in a story, male or female; and they seem to have been taken over from the Italian court entertainments, in which the highest nobility performed – incognito. There was even a convention that these amateurs should not dance too expertly, unless they were masked; that is, a demarcation existed between social and theatre dancing. The first dancer to appear on the Paris Opéra stage unmasked was Maximilien Gardel, in 1772, but the *corps de ballet* continued to use masks in grotesque roles until the end of the century.

Noverre was not the first to call for reform; in fact as early as 1717 the English ballet-master John Weaver had devised an entertainment at Drury Lane called *The Love of Mars and Venus* which can claim to be the first serious *ballet d'action*, as these productions came to be called. In Vienna, Franz Hilferding (who was Noverre's predecessor in Stuttgart) was working in the same direction, adapting Racine to the musical stage. Meanwhile his pupil, Gasparo Angiolini, collaborated with Gluck in extending the range of mime and music-drama, eventually going as far as to quarrel with Noverre because the Frenchman thought it was helpful to print the story of the ballet in the programme. Angiolini held that the dance and mime should make this unnecessary. In France a pupil of Noverre, Jean Dauberval – the creator of the original *Fille Mal Gardée* in Bordeaux in 1789 – carried his teacher's theories into practice, while another pupil, Charles Didelot, spread the doctrine over all Europe with his *Flore et Zéphire* (first produced in 1796 at the King's Theatre, London). This introduced two influential novelties – the use of wires for 'flying' and the wearing of tights by the men instead of stockings. Didelot eventually settled in St Petersburg, where he worked for twenty years, laying the foundation for the dramatic dance explosion in that city fifty years later.

But of more importance than machinery was the emergence of the dancer as a star of the show – and the female dancer in particular. For the acceptance of female artists on equal terms with men meant a decisive change: the leading ladies vied with the men as the centre of attention, and soon even outshone them. But men still had the upper hand in the theatre. In 1713 a regular ballet school had been set up by the Opéra. One of its first directors

Top: Gaetan Vestris, father of Auguste and himself a celebrated *danseur noble*. Oil painting by Thomas Gainsborough, *c.* 1780

Above: Auguste Vestris, with his son Armand, who also became a dancer. Oil painting by Adèle Romance, *dite* Romany, *c.* 1780

was the noble Louis Dupré and one of his first pupils to emerge from it was a young Florentine called Gaetano Vestris, whose talent and personality was to dominate the ballet scene to such an extent that he was nicknamed 'the god of the dance'. He was a spiritual descendant of Pylades, a *danseur noble*, and he handed on his talent to his son Auguste, who took more after Bathyllus, being an outstanding technician, somewhat stocky and short with dazzling speed and elevation. These contrasting styles have persisted ever since.

But the 'ballerina' (this Italian word survived in the generally French dance vocabulary, though its male equivalent, 'ballerino' passed for some reason into obsolescence) was emerging as the biggest theatrical attraction. Until 1681 all female roles had been danced at the Opéra by young men. But in that year, after a court performance in which the royal princesses had shone, girls were introduced. A Mlle Lafontaine is the first recorded lady dancer. Their importance grew, and by the 1720s two rivals had sprung into celebrity. Marie Sallé began as a child prodigy with a family troupe, and developed into a stately and dramatic dancer and also a choreographer (she arranged dances for Händel) and upheld a pure and virtuous public image, in spite of accusations of lesbianism and of appearing – in one of her own ballets, *Pygmalion* – in loose and flimsy draperies which permitted not only freedom of movement but voyeuristic opportunities. Her rival was Marie-Anne Camargo, a sparkling Italian-Spanish virtuoso. She too made a dent in the convention of female costumes by raising her skirts a few inches to show off her footwork, which was so brilliant that it was compared to a man's.

Both these dancers pushed the role of the woman – previously retiring and modest to comply with court etiquette – with vigour. They were followed by two ladies who did little for the private reputation of the ballerina – Barbara Campanini ('La Barberina') and Marie-Madeleine Guimard, whose exploitation of their charms became as famous as their display of talent. Of the men, Gaetano Vestris' son Auguste was the most celebrated – or most notorious, for he soon became as impossibly vain as his father; but the Gardel brothers, Maximilien and Pierre, also had enthusiastic admirers not only in Paris but in London, Stuttgart, Vienna and other big cities; for the art of ballet had already jumped across frontiers.

From the point of view of the future, the most important victim of the fashion for ballet was Russia. The Empress Catherine's enthusiasm for France and her dream of creating a Versailles in the north made St Petersburg a profitable home for the Italian and French dancers who still dominated Europe; they found in Russia not only a generous patron but a warm and discerning public. In Berlin Frederick the Great encouraged ballet performances in his new Opera House; while Warsaw, Prague and Vienna all became regular calls in the principal dancers' tours (the idea of a star artist remaining with one company is very modern), and Stuttgart was a major ballet centre, especially after the arrival there in 1760 of Jean-Georges Noverre. London, with its rich patrons and lively theatrical tradition was the main attraction for dancers after Paris. There the theatres were purely commercial enterprises, with a flexibility and sensitivity to public taste which made them equipped for change in a way difficult for the continental court entertainment in which tradition held sway.

IX The Romantic Movement

Above: Maria Medina Vigano, wife and partner of Salvatore Vigano, with whom she carried round Europe the Neo-classical style to which Romanticism was the reaction. Wash drawing *c.* 1815

Below: The Sylphide appears to the hero – Marie Taglioni and Joseph Mazilier in 'La Sylphide', 1832. Lithograph by R. J. Lane from a drawing by A. E. Chalon

lexibility was certainly needed, for social and cultural change was in the air. Roman ideals of austere heroism were replacing rococo frivolity; and realism was ousting artificiality. The Industrial Revolution was passing power from the nobility to the middle classes who would soon take over to the sound of the guillotine, and ballet began to reflect the new ideas. The hero of Jean Dauberval's *La Fille Mal Gardée* was no mythical god but a cheerful young farmer's boy, while the Italian Salvatore Vigano devised vast dramatic ballets such as *Otello* and *Joan of Arc* which demanded heroic mime as much as dancing. Decorative divertissements went out of fashion and expressive *ballets d'action* came in; 'the Shakespeare of the dance' became the highest accolade for a choreographer, being bestowed both on Noverre (by Garrick) and on Vigano (by the novelist Stendhal).

Unluckily, virtually none of the ballets of this period have come down to us; a single trifle, the charming *Whims of Cupid and the Balletmaster*, arranged for the Royal Danish company by an Italian choreographer in 1786, is the only surviving scrap. Based on traditional ballet convention, but arranged before the invention of the padded point-shoe, which changed everything, they may have formed an interesting blend of what we now call classical and modern dance styles, emphasizing strength and virility for the men, plasticity for the girls; these neo-classical qualities were soon to be replaced by a totally new set of dance ideals consistent with a new aesthetic.

The Romantic Movement, originally stemming from Germany, is generally held to have been born at the Odéon theatre in Paris one night in 1830, when a verse play by the young Victor Hugo, *Hernani*, had its premiere. This revolutionary and rebellious production expressed a new mood of flamboyant aspiration. But the very next year another vital ingredient in the new trend found its way to the stage – the passion for moonlit mystery, for the dark woodlands of the north in which love and death embraced, as love and life had been united in the sunny glades of classical myth. Dreams of the vague and unattainable replaced practical visual rapture. In a single decade a trio of ballet classics, closely linked in style and subject, were to launch an aesthetic which would grip Europe for a generation and permeate the world of ballet for exactly a century. It was born in 1831 and would not die until Pavlova died, in 1931.

Curiously, it was an opera which lit the fuse. Meyerbeer's *Robert le Diable* can claim better than any ballet to be the ancestor of romantic dance. Nothing could be more remote from the heroics of Vigano or the cheerful acrobatics of *Flore et Zéphyre* than its story (by the fertile librettist Eugène Scribe), which blended religion, witchcraft and seduction. It involved at one point a night scene in a ruined convent – brilliantly evoked by the designer at the Opera, Pierre Ciceri – in which the ghosts of nuns who had broken their vows were summoned up from the dead to bemuse the hero by voluptuous dancing and lure him into accepting a fatal talisman. Whirling mysteriously in their white shroud-habits (under the newly installed gaslighting) the unholy temptresses fulfilled their task and sank back into their tombs, while a choir of demons filled the air.

In spite of some accidents on stage, the scene was an immediate success. The new tone was set and had found its perfect expression in the thin, pale young dancer who had led the sacrilegious revels, Marie Taglioni. She was famous overnight, and next year she was starred in a ballet specially written by her father to display her style, *La Sylphide*. Here too she was a ghostly seductress: this time, though the ruins were classical, the feeling was pure gothic and the setting was medieval Scotland – a country made fashionable by the novels of Sir Walter Scott and the (fake) bard 'Ossian'.

The role confirmed Taglioni's lyrical genius. As a dryad who lures a kilted young laird away on his wedding day, she skimmed and floated over the moors in new 'full-point' poses which seemed to lift her off the ground, ethereally symbolizing spiritual ideals in contrast to the carnal joys of marriage. But as the ardent hero (aided by a witch) at last clasped her in his arms, she shed her wings and died. The success of this gothic fairy-tale marked the end of stage goddesses and satyrs. 'Henceforward' wrote the famous critic, Théophile Gautier, 'gnomes, undines, salamanders, elves, nixes, wilis, peris . . . have taken over the opera.' He might have added that Taglioni (whom he adored, until the next ballerina came along) and her descendants had taken over the ballet. The original choreography (by her father) is lost, but a version made only five years later by one of his pupils, Auguste Bournonville, has survived; its simple and charming integrity and delicate poetry – as elusive as the heroine herself – is still moving, while Taglioni's gauzy white skirt, which happily emphasized her every movement through the air, was to become the uniform for ballerinas for generations.

The success of *La Sylphide* led to a work which dealt with a similar theme, *Giselle*.

It was conceived by a conjunction of poets. 'My dear Heinrich Heine,' wrote Théophile Gautier (who was a literary critic as well as a poet), 'when reviewing a few weeks ago your fine book *De l'Allemagne* I came across a charming passage . . . where you speak of elves in white dresses whose hems are always damp, of nixes who display their little satin feet on the ceiling of the nuptial chamber, of snow-coloured *wilis* who waltz pitilessly, and of all those delicious apparitions you have encountered in the Harz mountains and in the banks of the Ilse in a mist softened by German moonlight; and I involuntarily said to myself: 'Wouldn't this make a pretty ballet?' Calling in an experienced librettist Vernoy de St Georges, to help him, he produced it in three days. In 1841 it was launched at the Paris Opéra, with Carlotta Grisi as the heroine.

The story craftily blends several themes in the romantic canon – the appeal of innocence and the joys of life close to nature (derived from Rousseau's teaching) in the village scenes, and the now popular visions of the Eternal Feminine in both its aspects – benign in the ghost of Giselle and malignant in the cruel Queen of the Wilis in Act II, in which Giselle's moonlit tomb added a mortuary frisson which echoed the cloisters of *Robert le Diable*. Medievalry, sickliness (Giselle seems doomed to an early death from the beginning) and pathetic madness – a sure dramatic effect since the days of Ophelia – and a seducer-hero of Byronic glamour combined to make a theatrical compendium of telling power.

The effect was heightened by the music by Adolphe Adam, a very advanced score at the time, into which specific *Leitmotive* are cunningly interwoven,

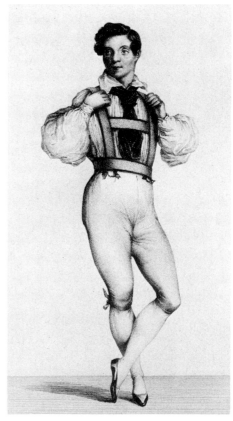

Jules Perrot, dancer, choreographer and husband of Carlotta Grisi, for whom he composed the ballerina's dances in 'Giselle'. Engraving by Konig from a drawing by Lacauchie in his costume for Filippo Taglioni's 'Nathalie', 1832

Watching Fanny Cerrito at Her Majesty's Theatre, London. Engraving from 'The Belle of the Season' by Lady Blessington, 1839

Above: caricature of Marie Taglioni in 'Flore et Zéphire', by the writer William Makepeace Thackeray

Opposite: Fanny Elssler in 'La Volière', a ballet by her sister Thérèse Elssler. Lithograph by M. Gauci after a water-colour by J. Defett Francis, 1838

and by distinguished choreography. The general effects were entrusted to the theatre's ballet master, Jean Coralli, but it is almost certain that the key passages in the ballet – the dances for Giselle herself – were by a far superior artist, Jules Perrot.

The reason for this was that Perrot was the guide and lover of the heroine, Carlotta Grisi, a twenty-two-year-old dancer from Italy who was the new sensation of Paris. Gautier, abandoning his adoration of Taglioni (who was by now nearly forty), lavished the cream of his formidable vocabulary on her: 'Carlotta danced with a perfection, lightness, boldness and a chaste and refined seductiveness which put her in the first rank', he wrote. She was the first of many ballerinas to make her name in this many-layered role, and the ballet spread across the dancing world like a flame; by 1860 it had reached Australia.

It clinched the dominance of the women in nineteenth century ballet; for though her partner was Lucien Petipa (younger brother of the future choreographer of *The Sleeping Beauty*), a dancer of great talent, his contribution was overshadowed. It is only in very recent years that the psychological and dancing riches in the role of the anti-hero have been explored. The sudden triumph of the ballerina was due partly to changes in social attitudes towards women and partly (as in most artistic revolutions) to a purely technical invention, the point-shoe. The little pattering feet of Camargo in her heeled shoes had slowly been replaced by heelless *directoire* slippers, and the device of invisible supporting wires had enabled dancers to seem to float across the stage since the end of the eighteenth century. In the 1770s a dancer called Anne Heinel was described as appearing 'on stilt-like tip-toe'. But the trick of stuffing the toe of the slipper with cottonwool (nowadays they are stiffened artificially) enabled ballerinas to perform prodigious feats of brilliance and balance and, with Taglioni, to combine them with noiseless leaps and poses to produce an effect of being airborne. The man became little more than a humble porter.

The demand for idols for male worshippers produced a remarkable supply. Taglioni was the first and the most celebrated, but she was soon challenged. Only two years after her triumph in *La Sylphide* a dancer from Vienna arrived in Paris who was to divide the new breed of ballet fans into rival camps. Fanny Elssler was a warm-blooded, provocative girl whose attraction was exactly the opposite of Taglioni's virginal allure – a fact seized on by the director of the Opera, Dr Véron who realized that a rivalry between the two would be good for business. Gautier, susceptible to almost any form of feminine charm, enjoyed them both. 'Mlle Taglioni is a Christian dancer . . . she flies like a spirit in the midst of transparent clouds of white muslin . . . Fanny is rather a pagan dancer; she reminds one of the muse Terpsichore, tambourine in hand, her tunic, exposing her thigh, caught up with a golden clasp.' It was Fanny whose competition drove Taglioni from Paris on a series of foreign tours (to the great benefit of international dance) and who, after triumphing in fiery numbers like a Spanish *cachucha*, gave a memorable twist to *Giselle* by her dramatic rendering of the part.

Elssler cannot be counted, strictly speaking, as a pure romantic ballerina; her lively sex-appeal echoed that of Camargo and could have proved just as

Right: Marie Taglioni and Antonio Guerra in 'L'Ombre', a ballet by her father, Filippo Taglioni. The heroine balances on a flower; the hero awaits her descent in white gloves. Lithograph by Bouvier after his own drawing, *c.* 1840

Below: Caroline Lassiat in 'Paquita', a ballet by Joseph Mazilier, 1846. Lithograph by A. Lacauchie

Opposite: Céline Celeste as La Bayadère in 'The Maid of Cashmere', a ballet by Filippo Taglioni, first produced in London in 1833; it had been launched in Paris three years earlier as 'Le Dieu et la Bayadère'. Lithograph by R. Miller, *c.* 1838

effective in eighteenth century roles, whereas Taglioni can hardly be imagined except poised ethereally in a swirl of Victorian tutus. But her artistry outstripped her period and she proved a healthy counterweight to the insidious refinement which was to overtake ballet in the later stages of romanticism, reducing it to an effete distraction fit only for extreme aesthetes or playboys in search of girls. The sickly look necessary for the fey heroines of these immaterial fables was all too easily acquired; underpaid, underfed and overworked, the death-rate of the young girls from diseases like tuberculosis was high; others, like Emma Livry, welcomed by Taglioni herself as a worthy disciple in her own style, died young from the risks of the profession – she was fatally burned after her dress caught alight during a performance, a night-moth who fluttered too close to the flame.

But several other dancers emerged in Paris during those crucial and exciting first years of the romantic dance. There was Fanny Cerrito, a lively charmer from Naples who married a French choreographer called Saint-Léon and became the principal ballerina of the Opera; and there was Lucille Grahn, a Danish dancer trained by Auguste Bournonville (who had been a pupil of Auguste Vestris in Paris before he returned to his native Denmark) and the possessor of both charm, physical beauty and an airy lyricism. Hans Andersen called her 'a rosebud born of the northern snows.'

Such a quartet of talent would make any impresario's mouth water and in 1845 Benjamin Lumley, the manager of Her Majesty's Theatre in London conceived the rich idea of presenting all of them simultaneously. Perrot, who was working at the theatre reviving *Giselle*, was entrusted with the diplomatic tasks of arranging a number which would display their different talents with equal effect, and Cesare Pugni (composer of Perrot's successful *Esmeralda* at the same theatre the previous year) supplied the score. Entitled simply *Pas de Quatre* it was so successful that it quickly became a legend. The forty-year-old Taglioni was indisputably the queen of the diversion, not only the most celebrated but the senior (Lumley is reputed to have craftily solved the question of precedence by proposing that ballerinas should appear in order of age, youngest first), but Grisi was Perrot's ex-mistress and Cerrito and Grahn – both twenty-six – were both established favourites not afraid of promoting themselves. However, the short number passed off not only peacefully but with sensational success; Queen Victoria (a faithful ballet-goer) brought Prince Albert to see it and it was widely illustrated, a true ideogram of the whole romantic movement.

Marie Taglioni appears at the hero's window in 'La Sylphide', 1832. Lithograph by J. S. Templeton from a drawing by A. E. Chalon

X **1859-1909 Focus on Russia**

The slow pageant of ballet down the centuries had passed from Egypt to Greece, from Greece to Italy, from Italy to France. But while Paris became the creative centre of the art during the seventeenth and eighteenth centuries, Italy remained the chief source of dancing talent. Milan in particular nurtured a whole batch of famous dancers deriving from the appearance at La Scala in 1837 of the Neapolitan-born Carlo Blasis. At the precocious age of twenty-three, while he was still chief dancer, he published his *Elementary Treatise on the Theory and Practice of Dancing* (1820) which codified a training system which was to become the basis of all subsequent technical teaching. This was followed by *The Code of Terpsichore* in which he expanded his methods.

An educated young man with a wide knowledge of the arts his teaching advocated a return to classical discipline and restraint. His work became famous; he was summoned to Paris and London and St Petersburg and his pupils were everywhere, from Cerrito and the American Augusta Maywood to the Russian Andreyanova and the enchanting Amina Boschetti of whom Baudelaire was to write: 'With finely pointed toe and smiling eye, Amina showers wit and ecstasy.' But after his retirement – or rather dismissal – as director of the Imperial Academy of Dancing in Milan in 1851, the mechanics rather than the aesthetics of his teaching took over, and it was the virtuosity more than artistry of the Italian dancers which continued to dazzle audiences all over Europe up to the end of the century.

By the middle of the century the fires of romantic Ballet had begun to burn themselves out in Paris and London. (They had never caught on in Italy.) Taglioni retired from the stage in 1847; Elssler in 1852; Grisi in 1854. Emma Livry, the frail young French girl whom Taglioni had hoped to see as her lyrical heir died, as we have seen, in 1863. What had started as a genuinely expressive art form began to turn into a variety of vaudeville, a convenient and agreeable excuse for the display of feminine charm. Drama declined into the girlie-show, sensibility gave way to sensuality, poetry to mass voyeurism. Apart from Perrot – brilliant but plain – the male star had disappeared. By good fortune a young French dancer from Marseilles was waiting in the wings to carry the seed of true ballet to a purer soil. Marius Petipa had worked in Belgium and America before arriving in Paris to partner Elssler and Grisi. One day in 1847 he received a note from St Petersburg: 'Monsieur Petipa, His Excellency Monsieur Gedeonov, Director of the Imperial theatres, offers you the post of *premier danseur*. Your salary will be 10,000 francs a year, with one semi-benefit performance.' This brief note signalled the passing of the ballet torch on its next lap, to the north. For sixty years Russia was to be the dance centre of the western world.

Arriving in St Petersburg, Petipa found himself working under his compatriot, Jules Perrot, and in 1862 after an interlude under Saint Léon, he replaced him as a ballet master (Perrot withdrew from the theatre disillusioned at the early age of forty-nine and lived quietly in France for another thirty-four years). He found a situation very different from that in Paris or London, one which was to influence the whole direction in which ballet was to move. The art had already passed through three phases – as a ritual ceremony under the Egyptians and Greeks, as popular spectacle and

Anna Pavlova in the Mad Scene in 'Giselle', St Petersburg, *c.* 1904. Though she did not die until 1931, Pavlova remained true to the Russian 19th-century tradition

Above: Marius Petipa, c. 1869. Though French by birth he was ballet-master in St Petersburg for forty years, and decisively influenced the Russian School. Engraving from a photograph

Opposite top: boy pupils at the St Petersburg School perform an arabesque

Opposite left: Lyubov Roslavleva as Aurora in 'The Sleeping Beauty', Moscow c. 1900

Opposite right: Virginia Zucchi in Luigi Manzotti's spectacular ballet 'Excelsior', c. 1881

entertainment under the Romans and Renaissance princes, and as an expression of personal feelings in the new democratic theatres of the eighteenth and nineteenth centuries. This romantic fashion had spread rapidly to Russia; Taglioni was dancing *La Sylphide* there in 1837 (to such acclaim that the ladies forgot etiquette and clapped their gloved hands, while some of the gentlemen cooked her slippers and ate them). In 1843 Gautier watched his beloved Grisi and Elssler dance there, with a *corps de ballet* 'unequalled in teamwork, precision and speed'.

But in Russia the opera houses of St Petersburg and Moscow were still directly under the Tsar's control; the dancers were as much part of the imperial household as the footmen, and the productions were paid for – with enormous generosity – out of the Imperial purse. Inevitably the style of entertainment reverted to that of Rome and the Renaissance. While technical standards of performance had to reflect the Tsar's superiority, the presentation had to symbolize his grandeur. Once more ballet took on the role of conspicuous expensiveness; spectacle was welded to romantic feelings.

To effect this difficult union needed a superb theatrical skill, and Petipa had it. While he was still only assistant ballet master in 1862, he mounted a mammoth production, *Pharaoh's Daughter* inspired by the recent excavations in Egypt, with impressive manoeuvres for a massive *corps de ballet* and a brilliant role for the Italian star Carolina Rosati. It was an instant success; Petipa had proved a provider of exactly the kind of entertainment the imperial court liked. Over the next thirty years he was to create no less than forty new ballets, apart from arranging the dances for thirty-five operas and reviving seventeen productions by other hands. (It is, for instance, his version of *Giselle* which has come down to us today.)

He had learnt much by working with the imaginative Perrot and with Saint Léon. He had a shrewd instinct for catching the public taste, a masterly gift of organization and planning, and the kind of active invention which could devise classical variations and geometrical figures for the *corps* in ballet after ballet. His audience-sense was illustrated by the lively and dramatic *Don Quixote*, which he arranged in 1869 for the Moscow audience – which liked works with plenty of colour and character – and the way in which he revised it two years later, with a more classical bias, for St Petersburg. His *La Bayadère*, written in 1877, was arranged to the same recipe as *Pharaoh's Daughter* – exotic settings for the first acts (India this time, with fakirs and an elephant) and pure classical dancing to show off the *corps* and the ballerina at the end of the evening. This formula, which gave openings for all sorts of dancers and for scenic and dramatic effects to suit all tastes, became the formula on which Petipa built an unrivalled reputation for two generations.

The material he had to work on was exceptional. The stars were still predominantly Italian, but Petipa – who had married a young Russian dancer – was eager to promote local talent. He created many roles not only for his own wife, Marie but also for a favourite pupil called Ekaterina Vazem, and he saw to it that the general teaching reached the highest standards of perfection. Petipa had himself been taught by Auguste Vestris and he was helped by an ex-pupil of Bournonville, Christian Johanssen, so the pure line of classical technique, as it had come down from Italy through France, was

passed on to Russia. Here it was joined by a stream which injected new life into it. Lacking supplies of trained foreign artists, local folk dancers had been recruited into Russian ballet troupes since the eighteenth century, bringing with them an exuberant and athletic style of male dancing far removed from the dignified graces of the academic ballet. The marriage between the two traditions produced a rich and vital approach to dancing far superior to the increasingly effete, ballerina-dominated manner of Paris, London and Milan.

The music for most of Petipa's ballets was provided by the regular company composer, a Hungarian called Ludwig Minkus; he was an experienced craftsman who could be relied upon to produce attractive and workable dance-music (a rare gift, as history has shown) but no more. Though frustrated by the stifling limitations of court taste, Petipa was no revolutionary, and it is unlikely that he would himself have made the giant stride needed to carry ballet out of the rut in which it had begun to settle. The same kind of mechanical theatre had established itself firmly in London (at the Alhambra Theatre) and in Paris (at the Eden), where endless rows of chorus-girls costumed to represent electricity, workmen in the Suez Canal, the products of the British Empire or the rewards of thrift and industry paraded their charms behind the top ballerinas of the day.

At this moment ballet might have subsided gracefully into the arms of music hall and burlesque if an energetic and cultured man called Vsevolojsky had not been appointed as director of the Tsar's theatres. He brought a breath of fresh reforming air into the scene; in particular he persuaded the famous composer Tchaikovsky, whom he much admired, to write a ballet for the Maryinsky Theatre (which had by now replaced the old Bolshoi as the home of the imperial opera and ballet in St Petersburg). The immediate fruit of this invitation was *The Sleeping Beauty* – a ballet which simultaneously set a glorious seal on all the traditional spectacle ballets of the past and opened up the way for entirely new developments in the future.

It is amazing that two men of such strong individuality and different ways of working as Petipa and Tchaikovsky could collaborate so successfully. Tchaikovsky had already tried his hand at a ballet, thirteen years earlier, with unhappy results. It had been produced in Moscow with an inferior choreographer who found the music unsympathetic; it was a failure and was quickly withdrawn. Its name was *Swan Lake*. Tchaikovsky, accustomed to following the outline of his own highly emotional inspirations must have felt misgiving at his new commission, particularly as Petipa worked in a very clear and dictatorial manner. He was used to preparing his productions beforehand in great detail, drawing diagrams, making little figures to move about, recording in advance every gesture and the exact measure and mood of the music which was to accompany it. These are the instructions which Tchaikovsky received for the end of Act I of the new ballet:

Aurora notices the old woman, who beats on her knitting needles a 2/4 measure. Gradually she changes to a very melodious waltz in 3/4 but, suddenly, a rest. Aurora pricks her finger. Screams, pain. Blood streams – give eight bars in 4/4, wide. She begins to dance – dizziness. . . . As if bitten by a tarantula she keeps turning and then falls unexpectedly, out of breath.

Rosita Mauri and Louis Merante of the Paris Opéra in 'La Korrigane', a ballet by Merante about 17th-century Brittany, launched at the Paris Opéra 1880. She was 31 and he was over 50 when they were photographed by Nadar or his son

Igor Stravinsky and Vaslav Nijinsky, *c.* 1912. The composer carries a monocle as well as his pince-nez; the dancer is in his 'Petrushka' costume and make-up; the photographer seems to have touched out the eyebrows

This must last from twenty-four to thirty-two bars. At the end of this there should be a tremolo of a few bars, as if cries of pain and sobs. . . . The old woman throws off her disguise. For this moment a chromatic scale must sound in the whole orchestra.

Tchaikovsky seems to have found this tight discipline a positive inspiration, and devised a score which appears to flow with total freedom. Petipa cunningly turned the old fairy tale (fairy-tale ballets were very much the vogue) into a many faceted myth which at the same time symbolised the majesty of the imperial court, and the spirit of youth and love conquering outmoded traditions. The sumptuous evocation of Versailles with its elaborate court etiquette paralleling the disciplines of academic ballet, or *danse d'école*, became the framework for glittering figures and variations, led by a virtuoso Italian dancer, Carlotta Brianza.

The success of the ballet (even the Tsar found it 'very nice') led to another work by the same composer, *The Nutcracker*. Petipa fell ill during rehearsals and the choreography was entrusted to his Russian assistant Ivanov; it was not a success, but Ivanov evidently had talents which might have developed; for he introduced a beautiful and very personal style into the only two scraps of his work which survive – the 'white' acts of *Swan Lake*.

It was this ballet – both the first (in its Moscow materialization) and the last (it was not performed in St Petersburg until 1895) of Tchaikovsky's ballet scores – which pointed the way to the future. It restored in full measure the romantic mood which Petipa had hinted at in his *Bayadère* dances of the Shades, and its tightly wrought libretto and symphonic score gave new emotional depths and aesthetic range to an often over-fragmentary art form. The history of ballet up to this point had consisted of fluctuations between two opposite tendencies – dance as an experience to be shared (the original Bacchic rites and the festivals of the Renaissance and Baroque courts) and dance as a spectacle to be watched (the Roman pantomimes and the professional displays of the eighteenth century). Romantic ballet had restored a sense of participation by involving the audience in the performance through a sense of mystery and emotion, but the grand spectacles which succeeded it had once more set up a barrier between the performers and the public. Now, through the art of Tchaikovsky, and Petipa and Ivanov, a balance was achieved. *Swan Lake* employs massive and splendid resources to touch the individual heart.

Tchaikovsky had died suddenly in 1893 before the revival could be mounted, and the second act was commissioned for performance at a memorial concert six months later. Owing to illness, Petipa entrusted the actual staging of the dances to his assistant; Ivanov's fluid, emotional choreography (danced then, as well as the full-length version a year later, by the Italian Pierina Legnani) launched a new approach to ballet – a vision of it as a real identification of music and movement, a medium of intense dramatic feeling and serious artistic content which would carry it far beyond court or commercial considerations, put an end to the domination of Italian virtuosity, and move its centre once more.

XI The Diaghilev Revolution

Opposite left: some key figures in the Ballets Russes at Lausanne in 1915: Léonide Massine, Natalia Gontcharova, Michel Larionov, Igor Stravinsky and Leon Bakst

Opposite right: caricatures of Nijinsky and Diaghilev by the film director Serge Eisenstein

Below: Serge Diaghilev, artistic director, impresario and manager, was the dictator of the Ballets Russes until his sudden death in 1929

The Vsevolojsky-Petipa-Tchaikovsky team had set a dazzling crown on the nineteenth century imperial ballet of St Petersburg; now another trio stood in the wings waiting to carry its art into a new century – Diaghilev-Fokine-Stravinsky. Like Vsevolojsky, Diaghilev had no practical experience in ballet (though Vsevolojsky did contribute designs and Diaghilev was to become an expert in lighting), but both brought to it wide cultural interests. Arriving in St Petersburg from a comfortable home in Perm, Diaghilev became a friend of two young students, Alexandre Benois and Leon Bakst; both of them were budding artists, while he was more interested in music – he actually took some lessons from Rimsky-Korsakov. In 1898, at the age of twenty-six, he became editor of a new magazine, *Mir Iskusstra*, founded to promote the symbolist doctrines fashionable in Paris. Benois and Bakst introduced him to ballet, and the next year he got a minor job at the Maryinsky Theatre, editing the theatre annual. But he quarrelled with the management and turned his energies to organizing art exhibitions.

These were so successful that in 1906 he decided to extend his activities to Paris (which he had visited as a young man with a cousin) and he organized a concert of Russian music there. This was so well received that in 1908 he returned with a whole opera company headed by Chaliapin to present *Boris Godunov*. It was a sensation and the following year he made up his mind to try his hand at ballet, a move encouraged by Benois.

Good dancers were by no means unknown in the West; Pavlova had been dancing *Giselle* and *Swan Lake* with a troupe from the Maryinsky Theatre in Berlin and Vienna only the previous year (1908) and the Italian dancers who starred in St Petersburg and Moscow were also regular visitors to Paris and London. What Diaghilev brought were new standards of production and a new idea of ballet's possibilities.

Diaghilev combined the qualities of the aristocrat, the diplomat, the connoisseur and the showman. Though not at first particularly interested in dance – his first loves were music and painting and his last love was books – he had a flair for picking choreographers and dancers, a passionate thirst for the best support that composers and designers could give them, and an almost diabolical instinct for the right mix. 'Ballet can only be created by the very closest fusion of three elements,' he declared, and he made it his business to seek out not well-known and experienced figures but young artists and composers who could contribute the newest and most exciting ideas.

The concept of 'total theatre' was not a new one – it had been put forward by Wagner a good fifty years before – and easel painters had been used on the Paris stage ever since Munch designed the sets for a Chekhov play in Antoine's Théâtre Libre in 1889. But Diaghilev's flair, and the thrust with which he presented the unfamiliar world of Russian art, made an intoxicating new brew of the ingredients recommended years before by Lully and Noverre. Within two decades he had overturned the whole concept of dance-theatre.

The traditional mould was already cracking in ballet as it was in the other arts. Isadora Duncan, a young and virtually untrained girl from San Francisco had challenged the whole ballet convention by appearing in Paris

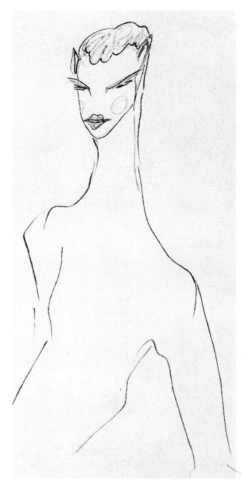

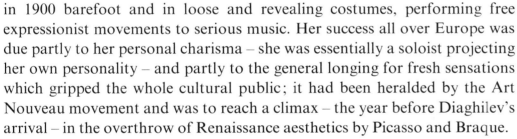

in 1900 barefoot and in loose and revealing costumes, performing free expressionist movements to serious music. Her success all over Europe was due partly to her personal charisma – she was essentially a soloist projecting her own personality – and partly to the general longing for fresh sensations which gripped the whole cultural public; it had been heralded by the Art Nouveau movement and was to reach a climax – the year before Diaghilev's arrival – in the overthrow of Renaissance aesthetics by Picasso and Braque.

In Paris another American soloist, Loie Fuller, had been exploiting the technical resources of the modern theatre in inventive numbers which were nearer to stage pictures or sculptures than to dance variations. In Moscow Stanislavsky had broken through the conventions of acting, and in St Petersburg Vsevolod Meyerhold was experimenting with productions which came close to ballet and preaching doctrines which were to be echoed by Fokine. Clearly the scene was set for a change. It came on 19 May 1909 when Diaghilev's Ballets Russes opened their first Paris season.

He started with his usual panache, courage and careful planning. He had obtained permission for most of the finest Maryinsky dancers to appear, from the prima ballerina Kschessinskaya downwards; he had arranged a generous subsidy from the Archduke Vladimir; and (partly through the impresario Gabriel Astruc) he had recruited in Paris an army of the society patronesses needed for any artistic enterprise in those days. At the last moment the Archduke withdrew (at the instigation of his friend Kschessinskaya, who was dissatisfied with her roles) but Diaghilev boldly pressed ahead; finding that the Opera was not available he booked the huge but

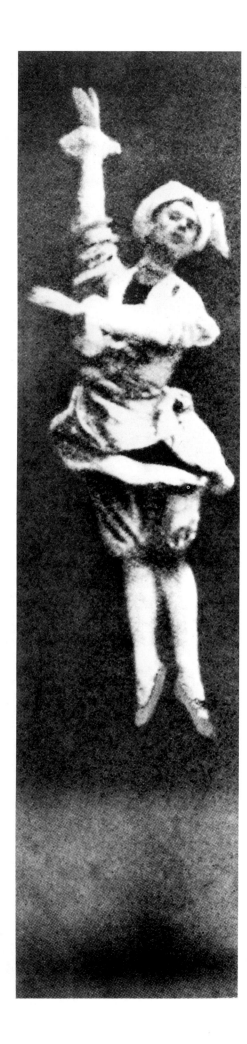

rather ramshackle Châtelet Theatre and proceeded to redecorate it throughout; he whipped up publicity through his fashionable friends; and he planned a programme which would show off to Paris the still unknown excitements of Russian music, Russian designers and, above all, Russian dancers.

It started with an already tried-out eighteenth century evocation, *Le Pavillon d'Armide* with Karalli, Karsavina, Mordkin and the twenty-year-old Nijinsky; proceeded with Fokine's virile Polovtsian Dances from Borodin's *Prince Igor*, with Bolm as the barbaric warrior; and ended with *Le Festin*, a hotch-potch of dances arranged to Russian music including items like the 'Bluebird' pas-de-deux from *The Sleeping Beauty*.

The result was explosive. In particular Bolm's savage and aggressive virtuosities in *Prince Igor* stunned an audience accustomed to the genteel trivialities of an art dominated by ballerinas. The pale dreams of the symbolists were deliciously shattered by a display of masculine ferocity (later *Schéhérazade* was to tap the same appeal) only to be appeased a few weeks later by the appearance of Pavlova floating and flying her way through *Les Sylphides* (composed by Fokine two years earlier under the title *Chopiniana*) with Nijinsky.

What Diaghilev had brought to Paris was a highly-spiced and super-theatrical echo of the fauve exoticism launched by Paul Gauguin twenty years earlier, with Tartary replacing Tahiti. At first he relied heavily on national flavour. His composers were predominantly Russian (Glinka, Borodin, Rimsky-Korsakov, Mussorgsky, Tchaikovsky, Glazunov); his designers were mostly members of the *Mir Iskusstva* circle (Benois, Bakst. Roerich, Bilibin, Korovin) and the dancers were all superb exponents of the Maryinsky training. Welding them all together was an inspired choreographer, Mikhail Fokine.

Fokine was responsible for all Diaghilev's first successes – *Le Pavillon d'Armide, Prince Igor, Les Sylphides* and (in later programmes) *Cléopatre* with the seductive Ida Rubinstein. He was to be creator of the triumphs of the return visit the following year as well – *Le Carnaval, Schéhérazade* and *The Firebird*. He was the ideal artist for a public breakthrough. He was a reformer rather than a revolutionary, who could carry his audiences with him into unfamiliar territory without shocking them or making them feel they had lost their way.

Working with Fokine was a young composer (he was twenty-seven when Diaghilev descended on Paris) called Igor Stravinsky, whom Diaghilev had spotted after hearing a single piece (*Fireworks*) in 1909. His first ballets (*The Firebird, Petrushka* and *Le Sacre du Printemps*) were colourful essays into his native folk-lore; they showed at once that he was an ideal composer for dance, with the springy rhythmic core which seems to be inherent in Russian music, a vivid sense of theatrical colour and the fertile invention necessary for the short-spaced structure of ballet – the finest dance-composer since Tchaikovsky.

Fokine introduced a new kind of dance-theatre; in place of the long, rambling picaresque narratives of tradition – pretexts for almost interchangeable exhibitions of virtuosity – he offered tightly-knit dance-poems with a single theme and consistent characterization. This involved a far more individual use of his dancers than in the old genre, and Fokine proved a master at developing and exploring the different qualities of each artist. Karsavina was the ballerina most in tune with his approach; her beauty, warmth, modesty and intelligence made her the perfect interpreter of *Le Carnaval* and *Le Spectre de la Rose*. For the already famous Pavlova, with her ethereal lightness and speed he designed *Les Sylphides* and *The Firebird*. (Disliking the music, she withdrew from this before the premiere.)

The men were even more astonishing to the French public. In Paris male dancing had fallen into such low esteem that heroes were often impersonated by girls (such as Franz in the Saint-Léon-Delibes confection *Coppélia* of 1870). Bolm was the biggest sensation of the first night, but soon he was eclipsed by Nijinsky, who introduced an altogether new style of male dancing.

Nijinsky, who came of Polish stock, was a prodigy even in the Maryinsky school. His combination of technical virtuosity and magnetic stage presence made him the most arresting male dancer since Vestris. Fokine, who was eight years his senior, seemed to understand his strange temperament perfectly and devised for him a series of parts which emphasized his seductive androgynous magnetism. In the first of these, *Le Spectre de la Rose*, he literally leaped into fame, and his compelling artistry was confirmed in roles as different as the stuffed puppet in *Petrushka*, and the half-animal slave in *Schéhérazade* (he seems to have been less striking in straight human roles).

His career was to be tragically short. He danced in five seasons in Paris and only four in London; the number of people who actually saw him was small and there is no film record of his art. Nurtured by Diaghilev (who was his lover) and miraculously developed by Fokine, he was a hothouse bloom who withered in the first cold draught of reality. Diaghilev dismissed him out of jealousy when he suddenly got married in 1913 and his career virtually came to an end. He was received back briefly into the company for an American tour, after internment during World War I, and danced for the last time in Buenos Aires in 1917. His mind was giving way – there was a family history of mental illness – and from then on, until his death in 1950, he was insane.

But meanwhile he had effected a drastic change in Diaghilev's repertoire. The nature of the Ballets Russes, and the demands made by their public, were very different from those in a state theatre like the Maryinsky. This was a touring troupe; it could not be expected to achieve the perfect uniformity and finish of a static company, but relied on stars, artistry and novelty. Attempts to imitate the triumphs of the Ballets Russes by large establishment companies are misplaced. The incessant routine of invention, surprise and topical creativity such as Diaghilev practised belong to the flexible itinerant troupe, and international stardom can be acquired only through travel. The stories of Fokine and Pavlova and Nijinsky would have been very different if they had stayed in St Petersburg.

But the built-in ephemerality of the company gave Nijinsky just the chances he needed. Fokine withdrew from it after a quarrel in 1912 (together with Benois, the gentle godfather and guide to its first years) and Diaghilev turned to Nijinsky as choreographer. The results were unexpected – a total departure from the Russian exoticism of the first programmes. Nijinsky had

Michel Fokine, the choreographer who shaped the first successes of the Ballets Russes. Portrait by Valentin Serov

Opposite: Nijinsky in 'Le Pavillon d'Armide' at the Châtelet Theatre, Paris, 1909, his first appearance in the West

Above: a group of the original dancers in 'Les Sylphides' (the Poet is missing). The unfamiliar positions show how fashion affects movement.
Below: Ida Rubinstein drawn by Bakst in the costume he designed for her in her production of 'Le Martyre de Saint Sebastien', 1911

been classically trained and was gifted with an exceptionally soft flowing style and a magnificent spring, but for his first work, *L' Après-midi d'un Faune* he devised stiff 'turned-in', almost jerky movements in which he left the floor only once. This short erotic episode (Paris found it shocking) seems to have been rooted in an obsessively literal translation of Greek vase decoration – two dimensional and hard-edged; played out against the lush emotional line of Debussy's music it proved a brilliant and original fragment, with Nijinsky himself perfectly cast as the detached, half-human but intensely charged faun.

His next ballet, *Jeux*, was equally revolutionary. This was an excursion into contemporary realism, with Nijinsky holding a tennis racket as he danced and his partners dressed in white sports skirts. It was not a success, in spite of Debussy's seductive score, but it carried ballet one stage further away from its romantic roots and its Russian stem. His next work ostensibly had a Russian theme but far outstripped it. *Le Sacre du Printemps* as conceived by its originator and designer, Roerich, was a piece of ethnic archaeology, but both Stravinsky and Nijinsky dug a deeper vein of primitivism. This was far removed from the sumptuous vision of Russia which the Paris fashion world had hailed after Diaghilev's first season, and like *L' Après-midi d'un Faune* it was received there with alarm. (As in the eighteenth century, London audience proved less easily shocked.)

It was Nijinsky's last work for Diaghilev. (He later produced, for the American tour, one more ballet, *Tyl Eulenspiegel*, to Richard Strauss' music but it seems to have been only intermittently successful.) His replacement in the company and Diaghilev's affections was Leonide Massine, a very different kind of dancer (from Moscow). His arrival heralded yet another change in Diaghilev's programmes, which abandoned the Russian element and adopted the sharp, witty Parisian style. Picasso became part of the Diaghilev circle, with an iconoclastic effect. In 1915 the company was putting on *Soleil de Nuit* with music by Rimsky-Korsakov and folksy designs by Larionov; im 1917 it mounted *Parade*, a Cubist burlesque with constructivist costumes by Picasso and music by Erik Satie which included the sounds of a typewriter and a hooter. Massine was not to tackle such a modern production again, until his last work for the company, *Ode*; but he mounted a series of very effective works in an individual style which carried on the old acrobatic tradition which harked back to the satiric dances of ancient Greece. Among his successes was *La Boutique Fantasque* (1919), *The Three Cornered Hat* (1919) and later, *Le Pas d'Acier*. By superhuman effort Diaghilev kept his company afloat through the war; what emerged was very different from his original glamorous spectacles, but it contained the seeds of most ballet developments over the next half-century. The new productions were partly based on Massine's own dance-style. He was not a graceful classical performer, but a character dancer with a wry compelling personality which could switch instantly from comedy to poetry, and a sharp, almost disjointed way of moving. The style – which had been foreshadowed in Nijinsky's *Faune* and was brilliantly exploited by his sister Bronislava Nijinska in *Les Noces*, which blended new ideas of space and rhythms with the old appeal of Russian folk-myths – seemed related to the Cubist idiom.

The formula for success now involved a fevered search for new ideas with which to preserve the old impact; the company and its stars were no longer a novelty and Cocteau could be sensed in the background after Diaghilev's desperate appeal to him: 'Astonish me!' A new company, the Ballets Suédois, had sprung up in Paris, with a director, Rolf de Maré, who was more closely in touch with the young art-world than Diaghilev. It had an even more avant-garde policy, illustrated by one of its ballets, *Relâche*, a Dada production by Picabia with a film episode by René Clair. Diaghilev evidently felt that there was a danger of losing contact with his roots, for in 1921 he suddenly went into reverse and mounted, in London, a full length, richly designed production of the old Maryinsky classic *The Sleeping Beauty*. This memorable event is often described as a 'failure'; but in fact it filled the huge Alhambra Theatre night after night for no less than thirteen weeks – a feat hardly equalled before or since. Unfortunately the initial cost was ruinously high, and when the season finally closed Diaghilev was deeply in debt. Had he had Pavlova and Nijinsky he could doubtless have extended the run long enough to pay off the capital expenses, but he was short of audience-drawing stars. For two years he kept going with short ballets many of which were marked more by their designs (by artists like Braque, Picasso, Utrillo and Derain) and their music (by Stravinsky, Auric, Satie and Milhaud) than by dancing. They included two brilliant ballets by Nijinska, *Les Noces* (1923) which reverted to a Russian theme with decor by Gontcharova, and *Les Biches* which was purely Parisian, with music by Poulenc and designs by Marie Laurencin. It was not until his last years that Diaghilev regained his choreographic impetus with the arrival of a young defector from Leningrad (the first in a long line), George Balanchine.

Balanchine was the last of Diaghilev's choreographers and a key link with the post-Diaghilev developments of ballet. His first major commission was to revise the Stravinsky-Massine *Chant du Rossignol* for a fifteen year old British dancer, Alicia Markova. This was followed at once by three outstanding ballets, *La Chatte*, with sensational transparent constructivist scenery and costumes by two Russian brothers, Naum Gabo and Antoine

Above: Enrico Cecchetti, teacher of the dancers of the Ballets Russes, as the Charlatan in 'Petrushka'

Below: Henri Matisse in front of his model for the nightingale in 'Le Chant du Rossignol' beside the choreographer Massine, 1920.

Above: Alicia Nikitina and Serge Lifar in the costumes by the sculptor Naum Gabo for Balanchine's 'La Chatte', 1927

Right: Baba Yaga the Witch in Massine's 'Kikimora', 1916, a design by Larionov

Pevsner; *Apollo* (with music by Stravinsky) and *The Prodigal Son*, with a score by Prokofiev and designs by Rouault. All these ballets featured a new male star from Russia, Serge Lifar.

They were important productions in many ways. The three principals concerned were to carry the Diaghilev tradition into three different countries – Markova (with Anton Dolin) to England, Lifar to France, Balanchine to America – and one of the works, *Apollo* was to prove the vital bridge, which Diaghilev had not yet found (though it was partly achieved in perhaps the first neo-classical ballet *Les Biches*) between the classical idiom of the old school and the modern style. When Diaghilev died suddenly (of diabetes) in Venice in 1929 while his company was on holiday, ballet in the west seemed to have received a death blow; but the seeds he had ripened were very much alive, and the future of dance was to be in the countries in which he had planted them. His funeral barge gliding across the lagoons can be seen as the last historic float in the pageant of dance. From then on each country was to have its own story.

Chucky

"L'APRES MIDI D'UN FAUNE"
(NIJINSKY)

4me Année.   No 16
15 Mai 1912
Numéro Exceptionnel
60 Pages
*
PRIX
1 fr. 50

7me Saison
des
Ballets
Russes

BAKST

Above: Alexandre Benois' original design – often amended later – for 'Petrushka'. The scene is the Buttermarket fairground in the centre of St Petersburg

Left: Bakst's design for Nijinsky in 'L'Après-Midi d'un Faune', which he choreographed to the score by Debussy in 1912

Right: Michel Larionov's design for Baba-Yaga, the witch, in Massine's 'Kikimora', 1916; the short ballet was absorbed in his 'Contes Russes' a year later

Fernand Léger, the French painter, designed this costume for a bird in Jean Barlin's 'La Création du Monde' for Rolf de Maré's Ballets Suédois, in 1923. The music was by Darius Milhaud

XII
BALLET ACROSS THE WORLD

D ance as a social activity and a public diversion seems to be an element inherent in human society, whatever the period or place. But the fact that theatrical dance is now accepted as an art form is due almost entirely to Diaghilev and his circle. Today there are few countries which do not pay at least lip-service to dance theatre as a serious part of their culture.

But the legacy which Diaghilev left behind is proving difficult to assimilate. One immediate result of his meteoric career was the spread of the concept of ballet as a shop-window of the avant-garde – an exceptionally flexible display device designed to show off the latest developments in every field in the most attractive setting. This aspect of ballet carried the obvious danger of a reversion to shallow entertainment aimed at a wide and inexpert public.

At the same time he lit such a flame of enthusiasm for the art that it acquired an international prestige. This more traditional appeal had been furthered by another pioneer figure who continued to operate in a direction very different from Diaghilev's but no less influential – Anna Pavlova. Pavlova was already an established star in St Petersburg when the Ballets Russes were launched in Paris, and temperamentally she belonged more to the generation of Isadora Duncan than to that of Stravinsky and Picasso. She remained fixed in the style of early Fokine – classical *danse d'école* with a twist to make it the instrument of romantic expressionism – and the fervour and interpretative genius with which she presented this form of dance made the troupe which she formed a missionary force which left an indelible mark in areas left untouched by Diaghilev's more cumbersome company. Then, as now, it was the charisma of a star performer which lit the new fires, though quality productions were needed to feed them. Country after country hatched the notion of founding its own dance company as a potentially mobile advertisement for its cultural wares.

The two-edged legacy has led to some awkward consequences. The Ballets Russes were a breakaway company, a touring troupe with no fixed home (though it had the use of rehearsal rooms in Monte Carlo for some months each year) no school and widely varied and uncommitted audience. Like a travelling circus it arrived year after year in the capitals of Europe bringing the thrill of a visiting show visible for a limited season. Flexibility, showmanship, novelty, variety and the immediate impact of star personalities were essential to an enterprise which had a precarious financial backing and so needed quick returns.

This operation was exactly the opposite of the solidly grounded national ballet companies which sprang up in its wake. These more resemble the Maryinsky company against which Diaghilev rebelled, with its solid material backing, its roots in national tradition and its school designed to ensure consistency and high standards of dancing. Their audiences are static but loyal and expert in a limited field, accustomed to slow developments and keener on quality than on experiment.

Some national companies today steer towards one aspect of the Diaghilev legacy, some towards the other. In the years immediately following his death the tide ran strongly towards experiment; some companies, notably de Basil's Ballets Russes de Monte Carlo, continued his rootless touring routines with success, relying on stars, nostalgia and novelty rather than on high polish, and everywhere the short ballet was in popular demand, whether the accent was on dancing (as with Balanchine's New York City Ballet) or on drama and design (as with Roland Petit's Champs-Elysées company). Slowly, however, the characteristics inherent in large permanent companies began to re-emerge in countries where they had been set up. The traditional system of feeding a steady supply of dancers trained in a single school into the company has shown its advantages (notably in Britain's Royal Ballet) and with it has come a popular swing back towards the full-length work which can display the all-over style and gives extra tests and opportunities to the principals.

It seems likely that both trends will survive – though the task of the touring troupe is complicated today by the fact that in large cities it is more and more competing with resident companies and often has to perform to relatively unsophisticated, provincial audiences who prefer old favourites to new ideas. But each approach has its role to play and it is fascinating to see the infinite varieties which they have taken on. Sometimes they cover new styles of movement ('modern dance' or folk idioms) sometimes they reflect new theatrical techniques (as with Alwin Nikolais) or a new attitude to music (as with Merce Cunningham), sometimes they involve the problem of injecting new life into the old classics. The aims and potentialities of the touring troupe and the resident national company will always overlap; disappointments arise only when they become confused, when the dashing itinerant aims at respectability, the guardian of quality apes the avant-garde or – the greatest danger – the stylistic variety of different countries becomes ironed out into anonymity.

XIII
Britain

Opposite: Margot Fonteyn and Robert Helpmann in 'Giselle' at Sadlers Wells Theatre, London, in 1937

Below: Adeline Genée, a Danish dancer who was ballerina at the Empire Theatre, London, from 1897–1907, where she is seen in 'Cinderella', 1906. She was naturalized, and became the first British ballerina of the 20th century

It is often a matter for surprise that the British are so addicted to dancing; the national character is presumed to be too cold and formal to permit such an activity. This impression grew in the nineteenth century when the unruffled English dandy became internationally fashionable. In earlier periods the British had been renowned for their sprightliness and their dancers much admired. It is more surprising that ballet – an art which seems to provide the perfect blend of high spirits and disciplined convention – only became endemic in Britain in this century.

What held it back was primarily the victory of Cromwell and the Puritans in the seventeenth century, at exactly the moment when on the continent the young Louis XIV was leading court festivities to their peak, and the replacement of the culture-orientated Stuarts on the British throne by a succession of stodgy German monarchs at a time when these festivities were being canalized elsewhere, under royal patronage, into national institutions. The masques so beloved of Elizabeth and the early Stuarts disappeared and during the Commonwealth years dancing virtually ceased; when it re-emerged it was not under the wing of the court but in the commerical theatre. London became a great showplace for dancers, but not a creative centre.

A few individuals fortunately survived to carry on the achievements of former years. The dances for the last great Stuart masque had been composed by a dancing-master called Josias Priest, and fourteen years later, in 1689, it was he who commissioned Purcell to compose an opera, *Dido and Aeneas* for the pupils of the fashionable girls' school of which he was by then director. Originally this work included no less than seventeen dance numbers; one of them was a solo for a drunken sailor which he presumably performed himself. Priest was only one of several skilled English dancing-masters who were in big demand on the continent; in return, Italian troupes were regular visitors to England, followed at the close of the eighteenth century by distinguished dancers from the Paris opera.

By this time the commercial theatres were well-established in London and at one of them, Drury Lane, there appeared the first important figure in British ballet, John Weaver. He was not only a talented dancer and mime but an adept producer, and in 1702 he mounted his first-work – a comic pantomime entertainment called *The Tavern Bilkers*. But he was also a serious theoretician. In 1706 he published an English translation of a new treatise on dance notation by a Frenchman, Raoul Feuillet's *Choréographie*; in 1712 he himself published an essay on the dance and in 1717 he devised *The Love of Mars and Venus*, which is the first recorded dance entertainment in which no songs or speech were included. In a preface to the programme he put forward principles which came close to those to be preached by Noverre forty years later.

The Drury Lane theatre (and one in Lincoln's Inn Fields) became a regular date for visiting dancers from the continent in the ensuing decades. In 1742 Garrick was appointed as its director and it was there that Noverre studied mime with him. But it was the King's Theatre which was to become the chief home of dancing in London. Sallé and Pierre Gardel appeared there and between 1782 and 1789 Noverre composed some of his greatest works for its company. It was rivalled by Covent Garden, which had been built in 1732

Maude Lloyd and Hugh Laing in Antony Tudor's 'Jardin au Lilas' (later known as 'Lilac Garden'), with the Ballet Rambert in 1936

by John Rich. It was there that in 1781 the two Vestris, father and son, caused such a sensation by appearing together that a sitting of Parliament was suspended so that the Members could attend the performance.

Such enthusiasm would hardly have been displayed for local dancers; ballet remained an imported art in which, as a rule, French artists performed French ballets to Italian music for English managers. There was a large and experienced dance audience in London, but no machinery for satisfying it with native talent. This situation continued throughout the entire nineteenth century. The stars of the Romantic ballet enjoyed triumphs in Britain (especially at the King's Theatre, re-named Her Majesty's in 1837) equal to those anywhere in Europe. Taglioni, Grahn, Grisi, Cerrito, Blasis and Elssler were familiar visitors. Jules Perrot was resident choreographer at the King's Theatre for six years, between 1842 and 1848, creating no less than nine ballets including his celebrated *Esmeralda*. Yet no school was set up, no academy founded, no charter granted by Queen Victoria, ballet enthusiast though she was.

Towards the end of the century ballet in Britain slipped into the same kind of decadence as elsewhere in the West. From a lyrical or dramatic statement it turned into a meaningless diversion in which the main attraction was a flourish of girls in spectacular settings. The Alhambra Theatre became, after 1870, the chief home of this kind of entertainment and from the point of view of sheer dancing London was less starved than might be imagined. Indeed, by a curious irony, an obvious derivation of Tchaikovsky's *Swan Lake* by the choreographer who had tried to revive it in Moscow, Joseph Hansen, was mounted in London before it was re-incarnated in St Petersburg. *The Swans* was put on at the Alhambra on New Year's Day 1884, and praised as 'a comedy and tragedy of terpichorean art'. The principal role was first danced by an Italian ballerina, Emma Palladino, and subsequently by a compatriot, Emma Bessone, who became prime ballerina at the Maryinsky three years later. Prudently, the choreographer abandoned the unsuccessful Tchaikovsky score and replaced it with music by the resident composer Georges Jacobi.

In that year a rival theatre opened in London, the Empire, offering regular performances of classics such as *Giselle, Sylvia* and *Coppélia*. Milanese dancers like Palladino and Enrico Cecchetti were engaged, soon to be joined, in 1897, by the Danish-born Adeline Genée, an enchanting soubrette who remained ballerina of the company for ten years. She retired in 1907 and was succeeded first by Lydia Kyasht, partnered by Bolm, and shortly afterwards by Phyllis Bedells. Kyasht and Bolm were outriders of the Russian invasion which was to drive out the Italians. A Russian company led by Kschessinskaya was presenting *Swan Lake* at the Hippodrome in 1910. Tamara Karsavina appeared at the Coliseum the same year and Pavlova and Mordkin in 1911. Another St Petersburg ballerina, Ekaterina Geltzer, was dancing at the Alhambra when, later in 1911, the full force of Russian ballet struck. The Ballets Russes appeared in London for the first time for the Coronation Gala at Covent Garden.

The almost annual London seasons by Diaghilev's company before and after World War II changed not only the art of the ballet but its audience. The productions put on by the Empire and the Alhambra had not been of the kind to appeal to the fastidious aesthete or the social snob; ballet in Britain had been a popular, undemanding entertainment. Now an appetite had been created for something different. Diaghilev's death in 1929 left a sudden unsatisfied hunger. He had created a keen audience, and the city now contained many dancers from his company as well as a number of teachers who had left Russia after the Revolution. The time was ripe for ballet to take root in Britain.

The seeds had been sown already. In 1920 some enthusiasts had founded, at last, a Royal Academy of Dancing; and in the same year Marie Rambert – a Polish pupil of Dalcroze who had been engaged by Diaghilev to help Nijinsky with the difficult rhythms of Stravinsky's *Le Sacre du Printemps* – had opened a school in London; six years later her pupils contributed a short ballet to a revue, *The Tragedy of Fashion*, by a twenty year old student, Frederick Ashton. In 1930 she gave a full dance programme at a public matinee. The Ballet Rambert was born to such acclaim that it was joined for a further season by famous Diaghilev dancers like Karsavina, Markova and Leon Woizikovsky. A few months later she founded the Ballet Club in her husband's tiny Mercury Theatre.

Meanwhile in 1926, another former Diaghilev dancer, the Irish-born Ninette de Valois (real name Edris Stannus) had founded her Academy of Choreographic Art, and begun to put in evenings of ballet at the Old Vic Theatre at the invitation of Lilian Baylis. The two small dance groups combined in 1930 to present some of the old classics and a number of new ballets under the umbrella of an organization called the Camargo Society, led by famous dancers like Spessivtseva, Lopokova, Markova and Dolin. The parent body was dismantled after three years, but Rambert's Ballet Club continued its pioneering work; Sunday after Sunday the hundred-seat theatre with its eighteen-foot stage mounted ballets by choreographers who have since become famous

But a larger enterprise was already under way. In 1931 Lilian Baylis decided to offset her people's theatre at the Old Vic with a counter-part in North London, and she invited de Valois to start a ballet group in it. In May of that year a tiny company, led by herself and Anton Dolin, mounted its first programme of ballets. Next year Markova joined as ballerina, and in 1933 Ashton became guest choreographer. Constant Lambert was in charge of the music, and in 1935 the company made its first appearance in a season in the West End. After it closed, Margot Fonteyn replaced Markova as ballerina. The team which was to create the British national ballet was complete.

During its first years its progress was not untroubled. Russian dancers still had a special glamour and the regular visits of the companies of de Basil and (briefly) René Blum could offer famous ex-Diaghilev ballets and an array of dazzling Russian artists. The Sadler's Wells company, as it was called, worked in a kind of isolation, which it turned to an advantage. De Valois proved the perfect director – shrewd, practical and forceful, but with a clear idea of her aims. She decided at once to found her company on the classics and a school and showed a flair for picking young collaborators.

Of these Ashton was to be of first importance. He had already acquired

Ninette de Valois, Irish-born founder-director of the Sadlers Wells Ballet (later the Royal Ballet) in 1962

John Gilpin with little 'Clara' in the
Snowflake Scene in the London Festival
Ballet's production of 'The Nutcracker',
c. 1955

experience studying under Massine and working in Ida Rubinstein's
company in Paris and in the demanding conditions of Rambert's Mercury
Theatre. For de Valois he turned out a series of ballets marked by delicate
musicality, wit, impeccable taste and fluent invention. Restrained lyricism
was his overriding characteristic and he implanted it in the company and
particularly into its still half-formed ballerina, Fonteyn. During the first
year before the outbreak of war, during which the company mounted several
de Valois ballets such as *Checkmate* and *The Rake's Progress*, Ashton
composed twelve works, ranging from the light, airy *Les Rendezvous* to the
romantic *Apparitions* (with Robert Helpmann as the half-drugged poet and
Fonteyn as his vision) and the sophisticated *Wedding Bouquet*.

If Ashton's gentle sensitivity set its print on the company, the nineteenth
century classics gave it a firm backbone. *Giselle* had been mounted in 1934 (it
was one of Markova's finest roles) as well as *The Nutcracker* and a full-length
Swan Lake. In 1930 it presented *The Sleeping Beauty* in a version which, like
its *Swan Lake*, was based directly on the notation which had been brought
out of Russia by Nicholas Sergueeff, former regisseur of the Maryinsky (he
had also supervised Diaghilev's production). The company could justly claim
to descend indirectly from St Petersburg.

It was not altogether a successful production but it established Fonteyn as
a superb classical artist, and it was with this ballet – with a sumptuous new
setting by Oliver Messel replacing the previous unbecoming designs – that the
company opened after the war in a new home, Covent Garden, and with
which it made its debut in New York three years later, in 1949. By now the
company had really grown up, with an unbeatable *corps de ballet* and a fine
team of soloists. The ballerinas have included, besides Fonteyn, Pearl
Argyle, Beryl Grey, Moira Shearer, Nadia Nerina, Svetlana Beriosova,
Antoinette Sibley and Merle Park, while among the men have been Harold
Turner, Robert Helpmann, Michael Somes, David Blair, Anthony Dowell,
David Wall and Alexander Grant. In 1962 the Russian Rudolf Nureyev
joined the company as guest artist and has appeared with them regularly
since. His partnership with Fonteyn became an international legend almost

overnight, setting new standards and arousing unprecedented public enthusiasm for dance in general.

The repertoire of the Royal Ballet is probably the widest of any large company, stretching from Petipa and Bournonville to Fokine and Massine, from Balanchine and Robbins to Roland Petit and Glen Tetley – a range which embraces modern dancing to electronic tape as well as pirouetting to Victorian melodies. Its mainstay has been the works by its three directors, de Valois, Ashton and (since 1970) Kenneth Macmillan. The last two have carried on the nineteenth century tradition in full-length narrative ballets like *Cinderella* and *La Fille Mal Gardée* (Ashton) and *Romeo and Juliet, Anastasia* and *Manon* (Macmillan), which together with Nureyev's grandiose *Nutcracker* have helped to develop the characteristic British style, lyrical and controlled with an aptitude for characterization and period and a gentle decorum which stresses perfection of detail.

In 1956 the company (which had also developed touring sections) received from Queen Elizabeth a charter which entitled it to change its name to 'The Royal Ballet'. Finally, and in the person of a company expressly founded to bring the art to the people, dance in Britain had acquired national status.

Other large classical companies were the Markova-Dolin ballet, which toured Europe and England successfully for three years with the classics and modern ballets, including Nijinska's *Les Biches*, and Mona Inglesby's International Ballet (1941–53) which concentrated on the Russian classics, produced by the former Maryinsky regisseur, Sergueeff. The London Festival Ballet formed in 1950 leads a peripatetic existence during which it has presented a wide range of ballets by many choreographers with foreign dancers who might not otherwise have been seen in London. Perhaps because its roving nature in some ways resembles that of the Ballets Russes, it has always been successful with Fokine's ballets (*Prince Igor, Petrushka, Les Sylphides, Schéhérazade*) and recently, under Beryl Grey's directorship, it has embarked on a policy of presenting the classics in versions markedly different from those of the Royal Ballet, such as its pleasantly old-fashioned *Nutcracker*, Mary Skeaping's *Giselle* and Nureyev's sumptuous *Sleeping Beauty*. The general dancing cannot compete with the Royal Ballet's in finish and consistency, but makes up by vitality and personality. It has had a distinguished team of imported stars – the most recent have been Eva Evdokimova and Nureyev – but its reputation was forged by its own dancers, particularly Galina Samsova, André Prokovsky and John Gilpin.

The steady growth of the Royal Ballet has inevitably pushed the Ballet Rambert nearer to the artistic fringe – a position it prefers. It outgrew the Mercury Theatre and it is homeless, but it has never lost its essentially creative character. While de Valois was tentatively establishing her company at Sadler's Wells, the Ballet Rambert was putting on a remarkable series of ballets, both by Ashton (up to 1933) and by another young discovery, Antony Tudor, who introduced a highly personal and sometimes revolutionary approach. He preferred little-known composers like Holst and Mahler as supports for pieces impregnated with strong feeling. In particular he abandoned the tradition of using his dancers as symbols or mythical heroes and heroines; his *Jardin aux Lilas* (1936) was about the private

Antoinette Sibley and Antony Dowell in the Royal Ballet production of 'The Sleeping Beauty' at Covent Garden, 1973

Top: Frederick Ashton's 'Symphonic Variations', performed by the Sadlers Wells Ballet in 1946, with (left to right) Moira Shearer, Henry Danton, Margot Fonteyn, Michael Somes and Pamela May
Above: David Wall in Ninette de Valois' 'The Rake's Progress', with the Royal Ballet at Sadlers Wells, 1966
Right: Frederick Ashton and Robert Helpmann as the Ugly Sisters in Ashton's 'Cinderella' at Covent Garden, 1965

feelings of real people, while *Dark Elegies* (1937) depicted the aftermath of a manifestly contemporary disaster. This new angle – which he was to develop later in America – proved a powerful influence on his successors. Another gifted choreographer was Andrée Howard, whose *Mermaid* with Pearl Argyle and *Lady into Fox* with Sally Gilmour revealed a subtle and sensitive musicality. At the start Rambert had depended on guest stars like Karsavina, Markova and Woizikovsky. But she soon developed her own dancers; Tudor, in particular formed a notable team of artists to interpret his style, including Maude Lloyd, Peggy van Praagh and Hugh Laing.

In the 1950s the company grew in size and mounted some large scale productions like *La Sylphide, Giselle* and *Don Quixote* (with Lucette Aldous) but shortly afterwards, when Norman Morrice became director, it completely changed its character, reverting to a small group, now devoted mainly to modern-style works. It was with the Ballet Rambert that the American Glen Tetley first became known in Britain, through such works as *Pierrot Lunaire* with Christopher Bruce and *Ziggurat*; and Morrice himself composed several ballets for the troupe, including *Hazard* and *Blind Sight*. Now directed by John Chesworth and Christopher Bruce, it continues a keenly explorative policy.

Christopher Bruce in Glen Tetley's 'Pierrot Lunaire' with the Ballet Rambert, 1967

While the Ballet Rambert still keeps some relics of its old classical heritage, the London Contemporary Dance Theatre is totally devoted to modern dance. It is an offshoot of Martha Graham's company in America and is directed by one of her former partners, Robert Cohan. It was born in 1967 under the patronage of Robin Howard, who had become an admirer of Graham during her British tour four years earlier. He founded a centre for the teaching of her methods – the only one in Europe – and it has become a focus, not only for the company, which has turned into a highly professional team which gives regular seasons in London and abroad – but for many visiting contemporary groups and dancers. Its repertoire is constantly changing, for the system lays great stress on creativity, but has a core of ballets by Graham herself, by Cohan (including a full-length work, *Stages* and the very successful *Cell*) and his pupils. Among the leading dancers have been Robert Powell (also from New York) Noemi Lapzeson, William Louther and Robert North.

A recent development in Britain has been the establishment of dance companies in the regions; the most flourishing is the Scottish Ballet, (formerly the Western Theatre Ballet) which is based on Glasgow and puts on ambitious programmes under its director Peter Darrell. The ballets include both modern works in the classical style, many by Darrell himself, and a few nineteenth century classics, such as the Scottish fable *La Sylphide*. Both Fonteyn and Nureyev have danced with the company in this ballet, and further distinguished guest appearances are planned for the future.

The Northern Dance Company is a more modest troupe founded in 1969 in Manchester, which has few ballet traditions, and it was severely strained by the recent economic blizzard. The regions are also served by the New London Ballet, which was founded by Samsova and Prokovsky after they left the London Festival Ballet in 1972 and offers strictly classical programmes of short new works by a small but select company. Classical ballet still draws the biggest audiences in Britain; but the younger generation is visibly attracted by the less formal language of modern dance, and it is to this idiom which most of the new choreographers seem to turn. Whether they will be able to forge a genuinely national idiom in it remains to be seen.

Ross McKim and Micha Bergese in Robert North's 'Troy Games', with the London Contemporary Dance Theatre, 1974

XIV
America

It is a brave man who foretells next year's harvest in the field of the arts, but the recent past is open to free inspection as a guide. Looking at this, there are obvious affinities between the state of dance in America during the last few decades and that in Russia in the nineteenth century – a comparison raising both hopes and fears. In both cases a large and eager audience and vast material resources attracted the best artists from abroad.

In both cases an earthy native tradition underlay the sophisticated conventions of imported ballet. In both countries an immigrant choreographer seized on the local style and vigorous home talent to produce an outpouring of remarkable works. The Russian George Balanchine in New York has echoed the achievements of the French Marius Petipa in St Petersburg.

The similarities are not exact. Tchaikovsky, Petipa's greatest musician, was drenched in the flavour of his country, while Stravinsky, Balanchine's favourite composer, was notably non-American. And whereas Petipa stepped into an already well-established company, Balanchine had to start from scratch.

For the history of dance in America is amazingly short. It is also unique, in that it has marked the development of two dance idioms almost simultaneously – classical ballet and modern dance. Of the two, modern dance (the label given to a variety of styles linked only by the rejection of the tight conventions of traditional ballet) really came first. There was a lively tradition of country dancing even among the Puritan immigrants, and its pioneers were touring from state to state before the first American ballet company had even been founded. Though it took rather exotic forms at first, owing to the personalities of its early practitioners, it is not unfair to see it as a branch of native American dance-idiom, earthy, demotic and home-brewed, a distant counterpart of the folk tradition onto which court ballet conventions were grafted in Europe. Now that performance conditions – which in the end shape any theatrical art – are becoming in many cases similar for both, the same kind of blend of a native and imported idiom which produced the Russian ballet style can be seen taking place today in the United States.

Significantly, modern dance sprang from the American soil in the far West, at the point most remote from European influence where the language of academic ballet must have been watered down to mere dancing-class triviality. It was at San Francisco that Isadora Duncan threw away her child's ballet shoes in the 1880s and started on her electrifying international career as artist-evangelist, preaching self-expression through natural movement. It was in Los Angeles that, in 1914, Ruth St Denis, a devotee of Eastern philosophy and oriental dance, opened a school with her husband Ted Shawn; and it was from the troupe operating from their Denishawn school that the two great pioneers of the modern movement emerged – Doris Humphrey and Martha Graham.

These dedicated revolutionaries (a woman dance organizer was in itself a novelty at that time) injected a new, serious mood into dance. It was a badly needed reform. The solemn representations of kings and gods had declined into frivolous and insipid music-hall entertainments. Fighting against lack of interest rather than fierce opposition, the two pioneers (there were others, such as the versatile Helen Tamaris and Charles Weidman, a gifted mime) slowly built up small but influential audiences in many parts of America in the 1920s. Humphrey, who joined with Weidman to form their own troupe, was concerned with gravity rather than with the aerial fantasies of traditional ballet; she used rising and falling, balance and imbalance, to express human conflict. By the late 1930s she had arrived at almost total abstraction.

The atmosphere in which she and Graham were working was that of the Great Depression – a suitable background for Graham's intense, dedicated visions. She had started as an exponent of the exotic dances invented by St Denis and Shawn (traces of them still appear in some of her ballets) but she had moved away, after leaving their company, into a highly worked out idiom in which the natural rhythms of breathing became the primary principle, expressed in terms of concentration and release. On this foundation she was able to build up a whole grammar of movement comparable to the grammar of classical ballet training – a vital step which translated modern dance from mere individual self-expression into a logical language capable of being both taught and developed.

It proved able to absorb the expressionism of the German modern dance – imported partly through an American tour in 1930 by Mary Wigman, who left her assistant Hanya Holm in a school in New York, and partly through Louis Horst, a musician who had been St Denis's accompanist, visited Germany, and became a strong influence on a whole generation of modern dancers – and to expand into Greek myth and abstract lyricism.

Graham had the luck to be not only an original thinker and inventor but a performer with a magnetic personality.. She soon moved beyond opposition to classical ballet (which she later came to admire) into purely constructive creativity, and the long list of ballets which she wrote for herself and her company – mostly with serious subjects and often laced with Freudian psychology – have become an important part of American dance history.

A number of creative sparks have been thrown off by this determined dynamo. Among them have been José Limon, the Mexican-born creator of the popular *Moor's Pavane*; Merce Cunningham, who carried dance into the avant-garde art scene of New York at its most inventive period, often in collaboration with the composer John Cage and, at first, the artist Robert Rauschenberg and later his colleague, Jasper Johns; Paul Taylor, a highly individual dancer and choreographer who mixes classicism and modern movement, comedy and solemnity in original blends; Alvin Ailey, whose mainly Negro company happily bridges the gap between art and entertainment; Alwin Nikolais who uses his dancers as elements in visual theatre. These – and other choreographers like Murray Louis, Anna Sokolow and Twyla Tharp – have dug a channel which carries the dance current in many new directions, some straying far from the old concept of dance-theatre, others converging towards the traditional mainstream.

The modern movement had a short headstart in America over the classical ballet, which did not put down local roots until the late 1930s. Though it is actually a hundred years older than St Petersburg, New York did not develop a theatrical life in the same way as that city; the impetus provided by a local ruler trying to imitate Versailles was missing. There was some dance activity, and the name of one performer has survived from the eighteenth century, John Durang. But it was only in the nineteenth century, when communications between Europe and America became easier, that ballet really came to life in the States. An American ballerina, Augusta Maywood (trained in Philadelphia) enjoyed considerable success in the opera houses of Paris, Vienna and Milan in the first half of the century and some of the top dancers from Paris and London, such as Elssler and Petipa, toured her country in return.

At the beginning of this century visitors became even more frequent. Pavlova and Mordkin made extensive tours and were followed (during World War I) by Diaghilev's Ballets Russes with Spessivtseva, Nijinsky and Massine. In the aftermath of the war and the Russian Revolution, several dancers settled in America. Fokine was working in New York, where he formed a short-lived company, and Bolm laid the foundations of today's companies in Chicago and San Francisco. In the 1930s these two companies (by now directed by Ruth Page and Lew Christiansen respectively), together with Catherine Littlefield's Philadelphia Ballet were precariously established.

Meanwhile an even more portentous venture had been embarked on in New York. In 1934 two wealthy ballet-lovers, Lincoln Kirstein and Edward Warburg, invited George Balanchine, who had just started a company of his own in France, to come over to America to start a company there. His School of American Ballet opened the same year and soon after the American Ballet Company was launched, operating in relatively grand style in the Metropolitan Opera House. It quickly ran into difficulties and in 1938 it closed.

The outbreak of the 1939 war brought about a drastic improvement in the tentative foothold of ballet in America. Colonel de Basil's company had arrived the year before for an extensive tour, with programmes which showed to audiences throughout the country that the classical idiom was capable of other styles than that of *Swan Lake* or *The Nutcracker*. Its return to Europe had to be cancelled in 1939, and it became based in America, slowly losing its Russian character. The departure of Massine in 1942 and the creation for the company of Agnes de Mille's *Rodeo* – an egregiously native product – marked the beginning of a steady Americanization, with increasing use of local dancers, choreographers and composers. Control of the company passed out of de Basil's hands and it carried on as a touring troupe until 1962, declining in prestige but acting as a focus for the classical tradition.

One of the reasons for its eclipse was the birth of a second New York company under Balanchine. In 1946 he had formed a Ballet Society for occasional subscription performances; in 1948 this acquired a permanent home in the New York City Centre and changed its title to the name by which it is known today, the New York City Ballet. Its success in the thirty years since its birth is the more remarkable because it has followed a new pattern. There had been many troupes assembled round the talents of one or two performers; but this one was specially designed for the interpretations of the creations of a single choreographer.

With the traditions of the Maryinsky theatre behind him, Balanchine set out methodically to fashion the perfect instrument, with a school to shape the dancers he aimed at; they were a new breed compounded of a mixture of

Ruth St Denis, the pioneer of modern dance in America, in characteristic Indian costume in the Dance of the Five Senses from 'The Temple', produced in London in 1908

George Balanchine, founder-director of the New York City Ballet, *c.* 1965

Three of Isadora Duncan's pupils as the
Three Graces, c. 1910

Imperial elegance and athletic, high-kicking, long legged showgirls – echoes
of the chorus line which had evidently fascinated him on his arrival in New
York. He did not demand interpretative intensity or dramatic personality;
on the contrary his ideals have presented the next twist in the classical-
romantic spiral by which dance, like all the arts, pushes forwards into the
future. As Petipa had reacted against the expressive styles of Perrot, and
Fokine had rebelled against Petipa's formalism, so Balanchine has gone
back, in his maturity, to classical coolness.

His taut authoritarian approach, which is combined with a super-sensitive
musicality and an inexhaustible flow of invention, has produced an awe-
inspiring roster of over one hundred ballets. He thrives on novelty (a legacy
from Diaghilev, perhaps) and though fastidious in many ways, he has never
been afraid of the ephemeral or half-successful. The reward has been a cluster
of master-works which will survive when the rest are forgotten – works
ranging from a dramatic ballet like *The Prodigal Son* to the martini-clear
Apollo – as sharp yet resonant as a Parnassian poem – or the pure musical
'*correspondences*' (to use Rimbaud's phrase) in abstract works like *Agon* or
Concerto Barocco.

Balanchine's ballets are usually nearer to orchestral ensembles than to
instrumental concertos and he has patiently avoided the traditional approach
which uses a dancer's theatrical impact as well as her (or his) dance technique.
He has not aimed at fostering stars but he has produced a superbly trained
team led by a succession of fine dancers who have included Maria Tallchief,
Tanaquil Le Clerq, Melissa Hayden, Diana Adams, Violette Verdy, Suzanne
Farrell, Patricia Wilde and Gelsey Kirkland, and, among the men, Edward
Villella, Jacques d'Amboise and Helgi Tomasson. He has also from time to
time employed dancers from outside such as André Eglevsky, Hugh Laing,
Erik Bruhn (the 'Great Dane'), and Peter Martins. The girls are noted for
their speed and attack, with more emphasis on the legs than on the upper part
of the body – an extreme departure from dance tradition down the centuries.
Another change from the Fokine approach has been the emphasis on
ballerinas as opposed to the male dancers.

Balanchine's reaction against Fokine's neo-romanticism has left a deep
mark on the American approach to dance, which is far more physical than in
Europe. Both performance and criticism tend to concentrate on muscular
action rather than on interpretation – a trend which seems to be rooted in the
practical Positivist philosophy which lies behind much American art.

The qualities of Balanchine's company are those of the finely bred
racehorse shaped for a special function. Its rival troupe in New York has
been a more all-round team. American Ballet Theatre was founded in 1939
with a deliberately eclectic policy which was exactly the opposite to that of
the New York City Ballet. It included from the beginning foreign choreographers like Fokine, Nijinska, Massine and the English Antony Tudor and
foreign dancers such as Markova, Dolin, Hugh Laing and Alicia Alonso. In
1945 Lucia Chase and Oliver Smith took on the direction from Robert
Pleasant and continued the varied policy, with a repertoire which included
nineteenth century classics like *Swan Lake* and *Giselle* done in the traditional
style (which Balanchine's company has moved away from), some of

Above: a Shakers' dance near Lebanon. Lithograph by N. Currier, mid-19th century

Left: 'Fancy Free', a ballet by Jerome Robbins for American Ballet Theatre, 1944. Robbins, John Kriza and Harold Lang

Overleaf: Sallie Wilson in Agnes de Mille's 'Fall River Legend' for American Ballet Theatre, 1948

Left: Martha Graham and Bertram Ross in 'Night Journey', *c.* 1958
Above: Balanchine's 'Agon'

Top: Judith Jamison and John Parks in 'Mary Lou's Mass', with the Alvin Ailey Dance Theatre, 1973

Diaghilev's ballets, and a stream of new works by many choreographers.

The most notable of these have been by Tudor, who developed in America the psychological ballets which he had inaugurated for Rambert in London, with such works as *Pillar of Fire* and *Undertow* (which introduced a striking dramatic dancer, Norah Kaye). The second talent to emerge from the American Ballet Theatre was Jerome Robbins, the first notable American choreographer in the classical idiom. Agnes de Mille had already shown the way, but his witty *Fancy Free*, to a score by the young Leonard Bernstein, showed at its first appearance in 1944 that he was an exceptional choreographer in a new and unmistakably American style. He has gone on to create many ballets with many companies, including musicals such as *West Side Story*. Among his biggest successes have been *Afternoon of a Faun*, a practice-studio rewrite of the old Nijinsky work which revolves round balletic narcissism, and *Dances at a Gathering* for the New York City Ballet, a miraculously inventive chain of dances to Chopin piano music.

With no steady base, a school which is not closely interlocked into the company and only intermittent seasons, American Ballet Theatre has gone through some difficult times; in finish and artistic consistency it could not compete with the New York City Ballet. But recently the slow logic of the theatre has begun to tip the balance in its favour. It is both more theatrical and more flexible than Balanchine's specialist troupe, better equipped to move with changing fashions. Frankly depending on the age-old appeal of the star performer, it has been able to take advantage of the arrival in the West of dancers from the Kirov company such as Makarova and Baryshnikov and to use as guest artist the ubiquitously compelling Nureyev. The result has been a dramatic rise in general standards (assisted by the engagement of Tudor as assistant director), the attraction of the stars themselves, and the emergence, in a new competitive atmosphere, of some outstanding native dancers such as Cynthia Gregory, Gelsey Kirkland, Fernando Bujones and Eleanor d'Antuono.

In a country now seething with dance activity – dance is even recognized in university education, with far-reaching results – a host of smaller ballet companies either flourish or at least survive. Among these are the Robert Joffrey Ballet – another mixed repertoire group, based on the New York City Centre (left free when the New York City Ballet moved to the State Theatre in the Lincoln Centre in 1964) and Arthur Mitchell's Dance Theatre of Harlem, an all-black group with programmes stretching from Balanchine to Petipa. New York remains the dance centre of America but outside it there are also thriving companies in Boston, Cincinnati, Philadelphia and Salt Lake City.

Within the last decade America has proved itself as fiercely dance conscious as Russia ever was, with the extra advantage of a free exchange of artists and companies and an active mine of creativity. New York is the dance emporium of the world, with foreign troupes vying with each other and with the local companies and a bewildering variety of individual experimentalists. This sudden flood of invention has formed part of the general art explosion in the last few decades. It has placed America at the top of the international dance league in this generation; it will be interesting to see how it will develop in the next.

Two Martha Graham dancers who started companies of their own: Merce Cunningham and, below, Paul Taylor

XV
Russia

Opposite: Galina Ulanova and Piotr Gusev in Rotislav Zakharov's 'Fountain of Bakhchissarai', first performed in Leningrad in 1934

Below: Vachtang Chabukiani in his own ballet 'Othello', created for the Georgian Ballet in 1957. He had previously been a star of the Kirov Company

Russia came late to the dance scene, but made up for the delay by her giant contributions since the late nineteenth century. In this period the standards of ballet performance at home reached new heights, while abroad Diaghilev made the words 'Ballets Russes' a symbol of quality and excitement.

The first recorded ballets in Russia date from 1727, danced by Russians under German management for the widow of Peter the Great. Her successor Anne, a great party-lover, set up an academy to teach six boys and six girls 'to dance in the theatre both sedately and comically'; this was the ancestor of the famous St Petersburg ballet school. Italians began to arrive under the reign of the Empress Elizabeth, and the Viennese Hilferding was engaged to run the Summer Garden Theatre. With the accession of Catherine the Great, friend of Voltaire and Diderot, contact between Paris and St Petersburg became closer, and dancers and teachers from the Opéra were engaged for her lavish entertainments. (A party, organized by her favourite, Prince Potemkin in 1791, cost half a million roubles.)

Under her son Paul ballet suffered a setback; he liked to see men only as soldiers, and he encouraged the debilitating practice of casting girls to take male dancing roles. However, only ten years after his death, in 1811, the famous teacher and choreographer Charles Didelot arrived from Paris. He had danced with Mlle Guimard and been a pupils of Auguste Vestris and Noverre, and he had earned an international reputation as choreographer with his ballet *Flore et Zéphire*; this marked a turning point in ballet in Russia.

Didelot remained for ten years, mounting over twenty ballets and, after a short spell in London and Paris, he returned there for the rest of his life. As a dancer he was not handsome – 'as thin as a skeleton, he had a very long red nose, wore a light red wig and danced with a lyre in his hand with great success' recorded a contemporary writer. But he was a fine choreographer, and a great teacher in the Noverre tradition. He laid the foundations on which the great St Petersburg company was to rise.

As in most countries at this time, the leading dancers were mostly imported from Italy or France; but Didelot's school soon began to turn out Russians who could rival them. One of the most beautiful was Avdotia Istomina, whom Pushkin described in his *Eugen Onegin*: 'She floats away, like some light feather on the west wind's breath.' This was the age of the romantic ballet and another fragile Russian star was Marie Danilova (one of the first ballerinas to dance on her points) who died of consumption at seventeen, after being jilted by her French partner.

Russia was fortunate in two ways. Its remoteness made the import of foreign dancers difficult and expensive; and it had a tradition of strong serf folk dancers recruited by early patrons like Count Matveyev (who, with his Scottish wife, had defied church disapproval by putting on dance entertainments as early as 1670). The result was a quick flowering of a whole generation of native dancers and the avoidance of the decline into effeminate insipidity which overtook most west European companies in the middle of the nineteenth century.

The great Romantic stars – Taglioni, Elssler and Grisi – had all appeared in

A characteristic scene from Leonid Jacobson's ballet 'Spartacus' with Inna Zubkovskaya as Phrygia, Askold Makarov as Spartacus and Robert Gerbek as Crassus. Yuri Grigorovitch produced another version for the Bolshoi Ballet in 1968

St Petersburg and Moscow (where a large and active company thrived in the rather more democratic atmosphere) and had built up an enthusiastic audience. Unlike most opera houses, Russian theatres already devoted entire evenings to ballet, instead of sandwiching them between operas. In St Petersburg the Bolshoi theatre was presenting every Monday, Wednesday and Friday, throughout the whole year (except Lent) productions by distinguished choreographers such as Saint Léon and Perrot, mounted in great splendour at imperial expense.

The direct interest of the Tsar in the productions had its disadvantages – imperial taste was conservative and imperial censorship was severe – but it preserved standards through a period when everywhere else ballet was in the decline. Jules Perrot, who became ballet-master in 1851, carried on Didelot's strict teachings. The company was being kept in trim for the arrival of the man who was to make it synonymous with style, Marius Petipa.

Petipa came to Russia in 1847 as a dancer, and remained there until his death in 1910. He was twenty-five when he arrived and already well-known; he had partnered Grisi and Elssler in Paris. But it was as ballet-master and choreographer that he was to make his name. His achievements represented in some ways a reaction against the teachings of Noverre, with their emphasis on content rather than on form, on feeling as opposed to structure. Petipa's approach was more logical and architectural. He took over the fashionable romantic subjects but he translated them into formal patterns. He liked to plan his ballets beforehand, sketching out with the aid of drawings and models entertainments in which solos and pas-de-deux, mime scenes, ensembles and character numbers followed each other in calculated patterns.

He invented a formula which proved flexible and theatrically effective, and he proved a master at inventing individual steps, enchainements and complicated geometrical figures to display the speed and virtuosity of his Italian dancers and the plasticity and vitality of his Russians. He was not poetic in the romantic sense, but his work had its own poetry. He knew how to make a pearl shine by surrounding it with diamonds and his range was wide, from the sparkle of *The Sleeping Beauty* to the vigour of *Don Quixote* or the mysterious serenity of the *Bayadère* 'shades'.

But in his last years fashion began to revert to romanticism. In his *Swan Lake* (a new version of a ballet which had been tried out unsuccessfully in Moscow no less than eighteen years earlier) illness compelled him to entrust the carrying-out of the dreamy second act beside the lake to his Russian assistant, Lev Ivanov. The result (first produced by itself in 1894 as a memorial concert to Tchaikovsky, who had just died of cholera) was a completely new style of choreography – plastic and romantic and seemingly growing straight out of the emotional score. For the full-length presentation Petipa arranged the two court scenes himself, leaving the completion of the 'white' lakeside acts to Ivanov. Unluckily these are all that remain as proof of Ivanov's talent; his *Nutcracker* had been a failure and the choreography has disappeared, and his other ballets have not survived.

But the romanticizing tendency which he introduced was to be taken over by Michel Fokine. Twelve years after the production of *Swan Lake* Fokine was arranging a solo for Pavlova called *The Dying Swan*. It was the direct descendant of Ivanov's expressive choreography, while the next year he was to go even further back, to the roots of romanticism, in his *Chopiniana* (later re-christened *Les Sylphides*) which deliberately recalled Taglioni's ethereal grace to music written by Chopin during her heyday. Petipa's retirement – enforced at the age of eighty-four after a failure – had marked the beginning of a neo-romantic trend in Russian ballet which is still evident today.

The departure of Fokine to Paris, together with Nijinsky and Pavlova and a host of others, was the first of many haemorrhages which the St Petersburg company was to undergo. Pavlova continued to return there after Diaghilev's departure until 1913, and Karsavina even after that – she was actually performing at the Maryinsky theatre on the night the Revolution broke out in 1917. Fokine himself went on working in Leningrad during the first years of the new regime. But the thread of natural growth was broken, and during the next decade the centre of Russian ballet began to shift towards the new capital, Moscow.

Moscow had a long ballet tradition, going back to the eighteenth century – the original ballet theatre was built in 1776 (rebuilt by an Englishman) and the school was considerably older. Most of the foreign stars had performed there and it had been the scene of some important premieres, such as Petipa's *Don Quixote* (in 1869) and the unsuccessful *Swan Lake* (in 1877). In 1900 Alexander Gorsky – one of the first St Petersburg dancers to rebel against Petipa's classical approach – was appointed regisseur to the Bolshoi company in Moscow and restaged many of the old ballets with alterations of his own, intended to liven up the dramatic effect. (His *Don Quixote* and *Humpbacked Horse* are still in the repertoire today.)

Ludmilla Cherkasova in the Bolshoi Ballet's 'Don Quixote'

Ekatarina Maximova and Vladimir Vasiliev in Leonid Lavrovsky's 'The Stone Flower', c. 1960

He remained in charge of the company until his death in 1924, and his approach still colours its style – dramatic, athletic, spectacular and broader than that of the strict St Petersburg classicists, qualities illustrated in a successful propaganda ballet *The Red Poppy* in 1927. The style was emphasized by its ballerinas, Olga Lepesshinskaya and Irine Tikhomirnova. Its prestige rose steadily and in 1944 Galina Ulanova, the star of the Kirov company in Leningrad, was transferred to it, at the same time as the chief Kirov choreographer, Leonid Lavrovsky, who became director of the Bolshoi company.

During the war (when the company had to be temporarily evacuated from Moscow) and during the decades after it, the best dancers in Russia were mostly directed to the Bolshoi, and with the firm establishment of Moscow as the Russian capital it became the chief national company. Its school, particularly under Adolf Messerer, won international fame and the first foreign tour in the West in 1956, made an overwhelming impression. The strength and plasticity of the ballerinas – Ulanova and Maya Plissetskaya among them – and the gentle virility of Nikolai Fadeyechev in *Giselle* were much admired. Subsequently dancers like Natalia Bessmertova, Ekaterina Maximova, Nadezhda Pavlova and Ludmilla Semenyaka have upheld the standards as well as the dynamic athleticism of Maris Liepa, Vladimir Vassiliev, Mikail Lavrovsky and Vyachislav Gordeyev. The 'Bolshoi style' emphasizes strong plastic backs, vigorous high leaps and a curvaceous line with frond-like hand movements which seems to reflect the art nouveau tradition.

The productions tend to be heavyweight. Lavrovsky's *Romeo and Juliet* with its wonderfully carpentered score by Prokofiev was even more successful than *The Stone Flower* by the same team. In recent years *Spartacus* by Yuri Grigorovitch – another Leningrader, who became director after the death of Lavrovsky in 1967 – emerged as a typical Bolshoi production, a renaissance of the old-time Hollywood blockbuster (which was itself based on the nineteenth century stage spectacular).

This style is sharply different from that of the Kirov ballet (the name given to the Maryinsky company of St Petersburg in 1935). The distinguished tradition of style and finish associated with the company was entrenched by the appointment, as head of the Leningrad school, of Agrippina Vaganova – an inspired teacher who set her stamp on the character of the whole organization. It has remained the most creative of the many Soviet companies. (There are over thirty scattered round the country.) It has produced most of Russia's recent choreographers, including Feodor Lopokhov, one of the first progressive artists after the Revolution – his Moscow counterpart was Kasyan Goleizovsky – Vachtang Chabukiani (*Laurencia* and *Othello*), Leonid Lavrovsky, Rotislav Zakharov (*Fountain of Bakhchissarai, The Bronze Horseman*) and Grigorovitch.

While Bolshoi productions verge on over-emphasis, even vulgarity, Kirov presentations sometimes incline towards a watered down version of French cabaret; but its production of *The Sleeping Beauty* and *Giselle* were wholeheartedly admired in the West and showed the special quality of the Kirov dancers – a pure line, musicality and a restrained and aristocratic bearing. Among their best artists in recent years have been the ballerinas Natalia Dudinskaya, Olga Shelest, Irina Kolpakhova, Alla Ossipienko, Alla Sizova and Natalia Makarova and, among the men, Konstantin Sergeyev, Rudolf Nureyev, Yuri Soloviev, Valery Panov and Mikhail Baryshnikov – a roster not to be outshone by any company in the world.

Unfortunately the Kirov company has been plagued – perhaps due to its traumatic dislodgement as Russia's top company – by erosion. Much of the best talent has been diverted towards Moscow, producing discontents which have resulted in dancers transferring (or, as the Soviet authorities call it, 'defecting') to foreign companies. This practice – quite normal in the West – cannot be compensated for by intake from abroad, and the result has been a thinning of talent. In the first years of this century Diaghilev had stolen away a whole stageful of stars – designers and librettists like Bakst and Alexandre Benois, composers like Stravinsky, choreographers like Fokine and Nijinska, dancers like Pavlova, Nijinsky and Karsavina. This was followed in 1924 by the disappearance during a foreign tour of Alexandra Danilova and George Balanchine. In 1961 Rudolf Nureyev opted to make his career in the West; Makarova left the company during a London season in 1970; Baryshnikov did the same in Toronto in 1973; and Valery Panov, after some difficulty, moved to Israel with his wife in 1974.

Galina Ulanova and Konstantin Sergueyev in a scene from Leonid Lavrovsky's 'Romeo and Juliet', first produced by the Kirov Ballet in 1940 with music by Prokofiev

These losses illustrate the difficulties of the new experiment which the Soviet companies are conducting – to shut out all foreign elements and exist entirely on their own native talent, using nothing but Russian dancers performing Russian choreography to Russian music in Russian decors. This reversal of the old 'free-trade' ballet tradition paid some handsome dividends at first but seems to be beginning to have serious repercussions. Apart from the dissatisfaction of individual dancers, artistic conservatism and the lack of creative urge (no Soviet ballet has won praise from Western critics since Lavrovsky's *Romeo and Juliet* thirty-five years ago) point to a dilemma which seems fated to become more acute. Russian dancers remain some of the best in the world but time is eating away at their repertoires.

XVI
France

France's position in the dance world is unique. For three hundred years after the great *Balet Comique de la Royne* mounted by Catherine de' Medici in 1581, both the nature, the development and the vocabulary of ballet depended on the French court, French teachers, French choreographers and French theatres. It was Louis XIV who set the seal on ballet as the diversion of princes, Beauchamps who laid down the basic grammar of classical dance, Noverre who showed how to translate it from ceremony and display into an expressive art and Dauberval, Perrot and finally Petipa who did so.

France also took the lead in codifying the language of ballet and fixing its structure. By the end of the eighteenth century the Paris Opéra was already a firm organization with a whole hierarchy of officials and a well-regulated supply of artists. This was invaluable during a long period, guaranteeing the conditions and standards of performances. But in the long run a price had to be paid for such solidity. Garnier's gigantic opera house, opened in 1875, was to become the symbol of establishment success – lavish but inflexible, floundering like a florid whale on the shifting sands of contemporary culture and weighed down by the trappings of tradition. The decline in artistry, creativity and prestige of the Paris Opéra Ballet after it moved to this edifice was accompanied by an increasingly conservative and deeply entrenched personnel, fixated on problems of payment and employment. This created an intractable block on which the ambitions of successions of directors were to founder.

The last major success of the old Opéra had been *Coppélia* and it can be seen as a portent. It was a superbly successful example of a decadent idiom – an unabashed piece of light entertainment, blessed with a sparkling score by Delibes, which suggested the combined pleasures of looking at girls and playing with dolls (its heroine teases an old man by pretending to be his automatic plaything); even the hero was danced by a girl. It opened in May 1870, and three weeks later the whole Second Empire society, whose values it reflected, disappeared in the military disaster of Sedan.

After this the fortunes of the Opéra declined. It was not until 1929 that they revived with the appointment of Serge Lifar as ballet director. Lifar, who had been one of Diaghilev's last stars, contributed his own fine dancing, engaged Russian ballerinas like Spessivtseva and raised a new generation of dancers such as Yvette Chauviré, Lycette Darsonval and Liane Daydé, while he presented both the nineteenth century classics and a steady supply of his own ballets. Some of these, such as *Icare* (which was danced only to percussion) were deliberately controversial; the best known was *Suite en Blanc* (later titled *Noir et Blanc*) of 1930, an abstract virtuoso display to a score by Lalo.

Lifar, who was an active propagandist with a striking personality, did much to restore the prestige of the Opéra, besides reforming its rather old-fashioned dance style. His directorship came to an end after World War II, during which he had continued, too willingly, according to his accusers, to work under the occupying Nazis. He formed a company of his own but was soon reinstated, and his standards have persisted after his final retirement in 1958, producing artists like Vyroubova, Claire Motte, Noella Pontois, Wilfride Poillet, Peter van Dijk, Attilio Labis, Cyril Atanasoff, Jean-Pierre

Serge Lifar. Etching by Louis Marcoussi

Bonnefous, Partice Bart and Michel Denard.

But the old troubles of administration were still evident, in spite of the drastic expedient of closing the theatre altogether for a spell in 1971. Under a new director, Rolf Libermann, the ballet company has recently won back much lost ground, with a rich repertoire ranging from the old classics to Balanchine, Béjart, Roland Petit and other French choreographers, and successful attempts to come to terms with the contemporary scene. This involved commissioning a full-length ballet by the avant-garde American choreographer Merce Cunningham, *Un Jour ou l'Autre*, in 1974 and the forming of a new modern-dance section of the company under Carolyn Carson, who had enjoyed a striking success dancing in this work and opposite Nureyev in Glen Tetley's *Tristan* to a score by Hans Werner Henze.

Meanwhile several companies based on Paris or Monte Carlo were attempting to carry on Diaghilev's tradition – that of the large itinerant group with no settled home or school but a colourful repertoire and a dazzling array of stars. Two of them started up almost immediately after Diaghilev's death – the Ballets de l'Opéra de Monte Carlo under René Blum and the Opéra Russe à Paris under 'Colonel de Basil'. In 1932 the companies merged under the title Ballets Russes de Monte Carlo, with a formidable repertoire which included many of Diaghilev's productions (supervised by his stage director, Serge Grigorieff). Among his dancers were not only famous Diaghilev stars like Leonide Massine and (later) Alexandra Danilova but a team of very young dancers culled from the Paris schools of old Russian dancers; they came to be called 'baby ballerinas'. Diaghilev himself had launched the fashion for immaturity by giving the fifteen-year-old British dancer Alicia Markova the leading role in the Balanchine revival of *Le Chant du Rossignol* in 1925, and now Tamara Toumanova, Irina Boronova and Tatiana Riabouchinska, with David Lichine's virile romanticism, became international favourites at about the same age.

The company's mixture of vivid personalities and varied programmes carried Diaghilev's message into far countries and over a difficult period. It was not content with reviving old favourites but mounted a series of new works by famous choreographers. Balanchine produced two works in a mysterious mood which he was never to recapture – *La Concurrence*, (which gave Leon Woizikovski a characteristic solo as the flea-tortured tramp) and *Cotillon*, a perfect vehicle for the black-haired, dark-eyed Toumanova. But the most important source of new ballets for the company was Leonide Massine. Recruited into his company by Diaghilev after the departure of Nijinsky, he choreographed his first ballet the very next year, in 1915. He became a prolific creator as well as a magnetic performer, and for de Basil he revived his *Three Cornered Hat* and also composed some charming light entertainments like *Le Beau Danube* and *Jeux d'Enfants*. He also embarked on a series of 'symphonic' ballets which proved highly controversial. He took not only Berlioz's Symphonie Fantastique which has a literary scenario but purely abstract works like Tchaikovsky's Fifth and Brahms's Fourth Symphonies and arranged vaguely narrative dancing to them. (Later he used Beethoven's Seventh Symphony in the same way.) The idea was not new – the French choreographer Deshayes had set a ballet to Beethoven's Sixth

Yvette Chauviré, ballerina of the Paris Opéra Ballet 1947–72

Symphony at the King's Theatre in London as early as 1829 – but it shocked many musicians. The ballets, striking in their day, have rarely been revived since.

Besides Massine, Balanchine and Lichine (who put on the entertaining *Graduation Ball*) the experienced Michel Fokine also mounted several new works, the most successful of which was a delightful chinoiserie Mozart ballet, *L'Epreuve d'Amour* with designs by André Derain; but he never achieved a major success in the new set-up – perhaps an even more compelling proof of Diaghilev's powers than the collapse of Nijinsky.

The company split into two in 1936, one troupe run by de Basil and the other by Blum (later by Sergei Denham), and choreographers and dancers vacillated between them. Amazingly, both troupes found enough engagements to keep them going for five years, during which the outbreak of war compelled them to take refuge in America. There financial and organizational difficulties proved too much for them and the last trace of their great achievement disappeared in 1962.

They had been only intermittent visitors to France and hardly affected the rise of several small breakaway troupes there. The first of these was the Ballets des Champs Elysées founded in 1945 by Diaghilev's former secretary Boris Kochno, with Jean Cocteau as presiding genius, Christian Bérard as designer and Roland Petit and Janine Charrat as choreographers. This was the first post-war company on the continent and it had the unmistakable flavour of Paris – taste, flair and invention. Bérard and a young Spanish designer, Antoni Clavé, introduced a new style of design, a decorative version of the agonized scraps and rags of the existentialist painters and sculptors; in works like *Le Jeune Homme et la Mort* (which arrestingly set a melodrama in a scruffy Paris garret against Bach's majestic C minor Passacaglia) Petit exploited the talent of a striking young dancer, Jean Babilée, with a feline strength and powerful personality; while he himself displayed a new genre of dance-drama opposite another big theatrical personality, Renée Jeanmaire, in a potted version of *Carmen*, boldly done to excerpts from the opera score. Gsovsky's version of the old romantic ballet *La Sylphide*, danced by Vyroubova among Bérard tartans, made as great an impression as Leslie Caron as the Sphinx setting riddles to Babilée in Lichine's *La Rencontre*.

In 1948 Petit left the company to form his own troupe, the Ballets de Paris, and two years later it disbanded. But its enormous success – its fresh youthful approach had attracted many of the best talents in Paris – had done more for the prestige of French ballet than most full-scale undertakings. Several attempts, besides Petit's own short-lived troupe, have been made to repeat the achievements of the Champs Elysées Ballet, particularly since André Malraux's effort to decentralize French culture; Janine Charrat had also briefly directed a company of her own, the Ballets de France, memorable chiefly for her own dramatic dancing in a madhouse ballet *Les Algues*.

Since its demise the most successful small troupe has been the Ballet Théâtre Contemporain founded in 1968 and attached to the regional arts centre in Amiens (it has subsequently moved to Angers); this laid much emphasis on design by easel-painters – now a somewhat outmoded idea – and lively youth-orientated scores. There is also an active company in Stras-

Renée Jeanmaire and Roland Petit in 'Carmen', a ballet which he devised in 1949 for his Ballets de Paris, using excerpts from Bizet's opera, with designs by Antoni Clavé

bourg, and in Marseilles Petit has assembled a troupe which puts on large-scale ballets of his own. In all these companies, as, to a lesser extent at the Paris Opéra, a very individual 'French' style persists, with an emphasis on elegant, spiky virtuosity rather than on expressiveness or musicality, and the slightly disjointed use of arms and legs which seems to descend from the Italian tradition. Ballet in France is, luckily, too deeply rooted to become anything else but French.

XVII
Germany

It sometimes seems that dance is a modern element in German culture; this is not so. The stately *basse danse* which formed the basis of most medieval court entertainments may have been Italian in origin, but the cheerful interpolations which enlivened it were often adaptations of the vigorous steps popular in the bracing climate of the north – one figure in particular, the Ländler. In this dance the gentle contact customary between men and women – normally only the delicate enlacing of one or two fingers – was replaced by an honest grip in which the man held the girl round the waist and then proceeded to spin her round. This revolving movement (which was later to turn into the waltz) crept into many early dance figures.

With the increasing sophistication of the small duchies which made up medieval Germany, imitations of Italian and French court entertainment became widespread. By 1600 pageants and processions were popular, and as early as 1654 an elaborate ballet *Le Pompe di Cipro* was performed in the Herkules-Saal in Munich by the nobility; ballets became increasingly popular there, and a French ballet-master, François Rodier was appointed in 1678. The opening performance at the Cuvillier theatre in 1753 ended with two ballets. Mannheim supported a high-class group of dancers, and Berlin became an important centre after Frederick the Great succeeded to his austere father. In 1744 he founded a royal opera house and two years later he engaged the Italian ballerina Barbara Campanini, 'La Barberina'; she was not overkeen on taking up her engagement, and had to be delivered by force; but, once arrived, she was so successful that she earned a three year contract. After her retirement a French ballet-master, François-Michel Hoguet, was appointed and stayed for no less than fifty years, mounting his last ballet when he was over eighty.

In Stuttgart the local company specialized in mime, arranged by Henri Malter and employing Italian- and French-trained dancers, and soon the ducal opera house was putting on productions to rival any in Europe, with French designers and the best dancers available; it nurtured the first German dancer to achieve success in Paris and London, Anna Heinel, and won a sufficient reputation to attract the services, in 1760, of Noverre. He arrived from Lyons, when he had just written his famous *Lettres sur la Danse*, which were actually published in Stuttgart and dedicated to his new patron, the Duke of Württemberg. It was in Stuttgart that Marie Taglioni was to win acclaim, before appearing in Paris.

It is curious that the Romantic ballet, though indelibly nordic in origin and feeling, and drawing entirely on northern mythology, left few traces in Germany. The ballerinas won the customary cheers and bouquets when they appeared in their favourite ballets there. But in general, ballet continued to appear only as a lightweight relief in programmes of singing and music. Beethoven's *The Creatures of Prometheus* of 1801 is the only substantial German ballet score written until this century.

The popularity and quality of opera is not quite a satisfactory reason for the delayed development of dance in Germany; after all, Italy could hardly be counted as less opera-orientated, yet it continually produced talented dancers and flourishing centres of ballet. Something else must have militated against it. This may have been the upsurge of democratic sentiments in the

eighteenth century which alienated the public from an art which – unlike the situation in France or Britain – remained totally associated with the court.

Whatever the reason, classical ballet enjoyed little popularity in Germany in the nineteenth century, and it was the arrival of an opponent of it, Isadora Duncan, in 1902 which lit the first sparks of enthusiasm. Her dionysiac expressionism and earnestness seemed to echo the dreams of Friedrich Nietzsche, a passionate advocate of dance as the symbol of human dynamism, and she was more admired in Germany than anywhere. It was in Berlin that she opened her first school in 1904.

It did not flourish, but she left behind a rich legacy, the movement which was to become labelled 'modern dance'. Several influences combined to produce this new development in Germany. In 1910 the Viennese-born Emile-Jacques Dalcroze founded there an institute for the teaching of 'eurhythmics', a system of translating sound into movement. At the same time a young Hungarian dancer, Rudolf von Laban, was appointed choreographer at the Berlin Opera. He produced a number of experimental ballets (some of them without music) but it was to be his theories of movement and his system of dance-notation which were to prove most influential.

One of his pupils was Mary Wigman, who turned into a solo recitalist with a strong personality and genuine invention in a strongly expressionist style stressing primitive emotions – she later toured in America. She in her turn had a pupil called Harald Kreutzberg who, after dancing in Hanover and Berlin, and working under Max Reinhardt, toured America with his partner Yvonne Georgi. These were all basically recitalists in the tradition of Isadora Duncan: another of Laban's pupils and his principal dancer, Kurt Jooss, became ballet-master at the Essen Opera House, where he wrote several ballets, including *The Green Table*, which won first prize in a competition in Paris. With this and other ballets of his own, he toured the world with his own troupe, the Ballets Jooss. Other group experiments in the modern-dance style were made in the Bauhaus art institute, under one of its teachers, Oscar Schlemmer.

Though never widely popular, this style of dance seemed firmly established

Marcia Haydée and Richard Cragun in Cranko's 'The Taming of the Shrew', devised for the Stuttgart Ballet in 1969 with music by Scarlatti arranged by Stolze

in Germany in the 1930s – but it was associated with 'modern art' and came under the official disapproval of the Nazis. After World War II it did not enjoy a great revival (though Jooss returned to Essen); its expressionism seemed outmoded and it was associated with the pre-war period which the younger generation was trying to forget. The odd result was a renewed interest in classical ballet – an art which had no recent connotations but which returned to the pure and objective theatrical theories of Kleist.

The first source of the revival of classical dance was the presence of the occupying forces. In East Germany the Russians guaranteed a stream of fine performers, while the Western powers – America, Britain and France – brought in their own companies to carry out similar cultural evangelism. Meanwhile Tatiana Gsovsky's school in East Berlin was beginning to turn out German dancers who could take their place honourably among the best foreign visitors. The dancing talent was there: the only difficulty was the over-dissemination of cultural energies – a situation inherited from the nineteenth century and encouraged by the occupying powers. This meant that while towns like the two Berlins, Hamburg, Wuppertal, Munich, Stuttgart, Frankfurt and Düsseldorf all supported ballet companies, none of them had sufficient status and resources to achieve international acclaim. Fifty opera houses with fifty ballet companies provided plenty of dancing, but no standard-setter. Another handicap was that some opera-house directors still considered 'serious' music sacrosanct, and would not allow it to be used in conjunction with dancing.

Then in 1961 the Württemberg State Theatre in Stuttgart engaged the young British choreographer John Cranko as Ballet Director (with a simultaneous interest in the Bavarian company in Munich). He set about building up a troupe based on its own school, he revised the nineteenth century classics to give it a firm stylistic foundation and he devised a steady stream of new ballets built round its three foreign-born principals – Marcia Haydée, Egon Madsun and Richard Cragun, together with two Germans, Birgit Keil and Heinz Clauss.

Five years later, in 1966, another product of the British Royal Ballet arrived in Germany; Kenneth MacMillan was appointed Ballet Director of the West Berlin Opera House, where he mounted some striking versions of the Petipa classics besides contributing new works of his own. Unfortunately he resigned in 1969, to return to London to take over the Royal Ballet, before his policy could be fully developed. The Stuttgart company suffered a severe loss when Cranko died suddenly in 1971 during the return of his company from its remarkably successful season in New York; his place has been taken by the American choreographer Glen Tetley.

But meanwhile other companies were coming forward. Hamburg embarked on an ambitious modern repertoire which included many of Balanchine's ballets, recently under the direction of another American, John Neumeier (formerly in Frankfurt), while Düsseldorf, Frankfurt, Hanover, Cologne, Wuppertal and other cities all boast active companies.

RUSSIANS IN THE WEST

Above: Natasha Makarova and Mikhail Baryshnikov in the *pas de deux* from 'Don Quixote' for a British Broadcasting Corporation television programme in 1975

Left: Rudolf Nureyev in his own production of 'Raymonda' for American Ballet Theatre in 1975. All three dancers were formerly members of the Kirov Ballet, leaving it in 1970, 1974 and 1961 respectively

The Bolshoi Ballet's production of
'Chopiniana', known in the West as 'Les
Sylphides', London 1960

The spread of dance-theatre across the world, and the recurrent changes in its focal point, have generated an extraordinary blossoming of companies in widely separated countries and, at the same time, left some formerly important centres relatively impoverished. Italy is a striking example of a country with a great dancing past and potentially a great dancing future but currently content with a secondary role.

From the point of view of continuity, Roman Italy had played a vital part in bringing theatrical dance from Greece and her colonies westwards. In the Renaissance period it was the pioneer in absorbing it into court entertainment and developing it in a style consonant with the other arts, thus laying a foundation for its future. Ballet today is descended in a direct line from an Italian ancestor.

The heritage was kept dramatically in view right through the next few centuries. It was a Florentine princess, Catherine de Medici, who introduced her native dancing into France in the sixteenth century and it was largely Italian dancers who performed it under her successors. Louis XIV appointed the Florentine-born Jean-Baptiste Lully (or Lulli) to be superintendent of the King's Ballet in 1661 and he became the Director of his new Académie. The first star of the Paris Opéra, Gaetan Vestris, was an Italian immigrant, born in Florence under the name of Vestri and founder of a family of ballet stars celebrated in France and throughout Europe. A fellow Florentine, Gasparo Angiolini, was working simultaneously in Vienna, under Gluck. The ballerinas were also predominantly Italian. Camargo (from a Roman family) Barbara Campanini ('La Barberina'), Marie Taglioni, Carlotta Grisi and Fanny Cerrito were all Italian born, while in Russia at the end of the nineteenth century it was dancers from Milan like Antoinetta dell' Era, Virginia Zucchi, Carlotta Brianza and Pieri Legnani who dominated the Maryinsky. When *La Sylphide* launched the Romantic movement in France in 1832 the decor was by Pierre Ciceri (from a Milanese family), the libretto of the ballet had been written by Filippo Taglioni and the 'sylphide' herself was his incomparable daughter Marie Taglioni. When Diaghilev set out to conquer the world with his new company he saw to it that his dancers were under the eye of the great teacher Enrico Cecchetti.

Italian influence on classical dance can hardly be overestimated. While the French tradition was cool and majestic, geared to royal occasions, the Italians introduced a quick, lively approach probably derived from the Commedia del' Arte. The two styles have become the *adagio* and *allegro* elements which combine to make the perfect mixture for any extended dance.

The Italian manner was practised all over Italy in the eighteenth century; Naples, Turin, Padua and Venice all had active companies. But gradually it became concentrated and perfected in one place – the school attached to the Teatro Ducale in Milan, which later took the name of La Scala. The foundation of this establishment was laid by Salvatore Vigano. He came from a family of dancers and became a celebrated international choreographer and performer, especially with his Spanish wife Maria Medina. They represented an austere neoclassical reaction against rococo frivolity, specializing in heroic ballets in which Maria danced in flesh coloured tights beneath loose transparent draperies which caused a sensation. Vigano spent

Italy and other Countries

Dancers of the Alwin Nikolais company in a typical production, 'Imago', which he devised in 1963. He often uses his dancers as moving pieces of scenery or 'props'

121

Two Italian Commedia dell' Arte dancers. Drawing by Jacques Callot, c. 1610

several years in Vienna, where he choreographed *The Creatures of Prometheus*, a ballet commissioned from Beethoven in honour of the Empress Maria Theresa. He returned to Milan in 1812 and arranged a series of ballets in a style which made use of large groups and complicated figures for the *corps de ballet*, in whose training he took special care. 'The patient, slow Vigano took the time to ensure that the very last member of the cast who was not sure of his role should dance it to perfection,' wrote the novelist Stendhal. It was this attention to detail which was to be the strength of Milan-trained dancers over the next hundred years.

If Vigano was the spiritual godfather of the La Scala school, his pupil Carlo Blasis was its founder. He had danced with the French artist Pierre Gardel (as Vigano had worked with Dauberval) but his real genius was for analysis and teaching. At the precocious age of twenty-five he published a treatise on dancing in Milan, and this was followed in 1828 by *The Code of Terpsichore* which laid down a system of exercises which have remained the basis of classical teaching ever since – daily practice planned to develop each muscle and facility in turn, always with an eye on a smooth and apparently effortless performance. By 1840 his fame had spread across Europe and his pupils were appearing everywhere; but in 1851 he was manoeuvred out of his position in Milan. The result was a series of travels which extended his influence from London to St Petersburg.

The second half of the nineteenth century saw the same decline in quality in

Italian dance as was observable elsewhere. Gigantic productions, such as Luigi Manzotti's *Excelsior* in Milan, provided tasteless but highly popular spectacles, while in Paris a special theatre, the Eden, was constructed for the production of extravaganzas exported from Italy. Artistically dance had reached dizzy depths; but the discipline of the Milan school survived, providing the world's opera houses with ever more brilliant virtuosos, ever more breathtaking new steps – it was Legnani who first executed thirty-two *fouettés* (in *Aladdin* at the London Alhambra in 1892) – and new technical improvements.

In 1923 Diaghilev sent the half-trained young Lifar, newly arrived from Russia, to Milan. But his professor, Cecchetti, was ageing and the balanced teaching laid down by Vigano and Blasis was turning into a training for circus tricks. The arrival of the Ballets Russes in Europe, bringing with them a return to old standards of artistry, had put an end to the domination of Milan, and ballet in Italy went into a decline from which it is only slowly recovering. Everywhere opera has pushed ballet into a minor role. Companies still survive precariously in Rome, Florence and Naples, and La Scala still mounts ambitious productions. But even there politics and social unrest have undermined the standards, and for the moment the great traditions of Italian dance are best personified in one or two individual performers such as Carla Fracci and Paolo Bortoluzzi, who became international stars.

Erik Bruhn, the outstanding Danish dancer of his generation, as James, hero of August Bournonville's version of 'La Sylphide', first produced in Copenhagen in 1836

Like Italy, Austria has a distinguished dance history which is only fitfully reflected today. In the early eighteenth century it was a ballet centre, with ambitious programmes at the court theatre and in the commerical Kärntnertor, and many celebrated dancers and choreographers worked there. It produced an eminent figure of its own very early on – Franz Hilferding. He was one of the first ballet reformers, starting the trend which took it away from simple hedonistic diversion towards dance-drama. As early as 1740 he was arranging ballet-pantomimes based on plays by Racine and Molière, with a strong emphasis on mime.

Ten years later he was in Stuttgart, where he further developed his theories and became an important influence on Noverre, who succeeded him. Soon afterwards (in 1758) he was summoned to St Petersburg where he helped to shape the foundations of the Maryinsky company. But on his return to Vienna he found that his place had been taken by the Italian Angiolini, and he died poor and forgotten a few years later, while Noverre reigned (for seven years) at the court theatre.

After Noverre's departure Vigano took charge in Vienna, and it was there that Beethoven composed for him (in 1801) *The Creatures of Prometheus*. Soon afterwards Filippo Taglioni became ballet-master and his famous daughter Marie made her debut there in 1822. This was four years after the little Viennese girl who was to be her greatest rival, Fanny Elssler, had joined the *corps de ballet*. She soon became a local star; in 1834 she conquered Paris and joined the ranks of the great.

The Vienna opera – it was opened in 1869 with a ballet by Taglioni's son Paul – continued as a centre of ballet till the end of the century, with local dancers slowly replacing the French and Italian visiting stars. As in

Robert Helpmann, who was born in Australia in 1909, as the crazy old Knight in Nureyev's production of 'Don Quixote' for the Australian Ballet, 1973

Germany, the modern-dance style replaced the classical idiom between the Wars, and it was not until 1959 that it returned to the *danse d'école* in *Giselle*. The company quickly grew to a size and quality which enabled it to mount most of the nineteenth century classics and it toured America in 1972; but recently the prestige of the company has declined. Like Denmark, Austria has the distinction of having produced in the past a great choreographer and a great dancer – with a swing of the pendulum it could well resume an important place in the dance world.

The history of Dance in Holland runs in the opposite direction. Until this century there was virtually no dance tradition in the Netherlands; then, suddenly after World War I, the scene changed. It began with a German dancer, Yvonne Georgi, a pupil of Dalcroze and Mary Wigman who had joined Harald Kreutzberg to give recitals all over the world. She became ballet-mistress at Hanover, then at Amsterdam where, in 1936, she set up a company. In 1958 it was taken over by the Russian-born Sonia Gaskell under a new title, the Nederlands Ballet, with Benjamin Harkavy as joint director. In 1961 it absorbed two other small groups to become the Dutch National Ballet.

Today it is a large company with Amsterdam as its home. It has a wide repertoire stretching from the Russian classics (often mounted by Russians) to modern dance, with many ballets by its present directors, Rudi van Dantzig and Hans van Manen and others, including Toer van Schayk. The small size of the country has enabled it to adopt a rhythm of short-range tours which has built up audiences in many small towns. It has also successfully appeared in Paris, London, Germany and Switzerland.

The emergence of a full-sized professional company in such a short time is impressive. Even more remarkable is the fact that the Netherlands also support one of the most active modern groups in Europe. In 1959 Harkavy resigned from Gaskell's Nederlands Ballet, together with some of the dancers; and formed the Nederlands Dance Theatre, based on The Hague. It adopted at once a resolutely experimental policy, and was lucky enough to find some talented choreographers in the new style, including van Dantzig, Hans van Manen, Glen Tetley and Jaap Flier. It has appeared with great success in New York, London, Paris and many other cities, introducing a style of dance which is neither classical nor – like many modern techniques – based on central European or Graham training. The direction of the company has changed several times, but its reputation is secure.

Not content with these two troupes, the Netherlands also supports a big company in Antwerp, the Ballet van Vlaanderen, and a troupe specializing in entertainment for children, the Scapino. In less than fifty years Holland has become one of the dance centres of Europe.

Belgium too has become actively interested in dance. Romantic ballet was already well under way when the country came into existence (in 1839) and throughout the nineteenth century Brussels was a regular date for famous ballerinas making a European tour. But it was not until recently that it became a creative centre with a company and a choreographer of striking individuality, Maurice Béjart.

Béjart is French by birth, and began his career in Marseilles before joining Roland Petit's company. In 1954 he formed his own troupe, the Ballets de l'Etoile, and quickly developed a personal choreographic style which stressed modernity while retaining classical elements, especially a sharp Parisian brilliance for his ballerinas. A powerfully sexual interpretation of Stravinsky's *Le Sacre du Printemps* led to his appointment in 1960 as ballet director of the Théâtre de la Monnaie in Brussels, which became the headquarters of a large company which has toured successfully all over the world.

Béjart has a slightly florid style in which he uses big names (Beethoven, Bach or Baudelaire) and grandiose themes as the basis for large-scale spectacles designed for mass audiences – he positively enjoys performing in huge arenas. He has a strong theatrical sense, skilfully mixing poetry, singing, extravagant costumes and all kinds of sound and music in mixed-media shows. He has developed an excellent team to carry out his own demanding kind of movement (which often involves oriental idioms), especially among the men, who have included dancers like Paolo Bortoluzzi and Jorge Donn. His productions can sometimes be vulgar but they are never dull.

The Royal Danish Ballet is rated as one of the top classical companies in the world, a position it has held for a hundred years. Kings of Denmark encouraged entertainment in the Parisian style from the seventeenth century onwards and it was a Frenchman who was appointed ballet-master when the Royal Theatre opened in 1748.

The Italian contingent soon moved in and in 1775 Vincenzo Galeotti was engaged. He remained for forty years and built up an important company, contributing many ballets of his own devising – one of them, *The Whims of Cupid* is still performed, the oldest of all surviving ballets.

He was succeeded by a pupil of Noverre, Antoine Bournonville, and he was followed in his turn by his own son August, who became the founder of the Danish national style – still referred to as 'the Bournonville style'. He had worked under Auguste Vestris in Paris and became a soloist at the Paris Opéra. When he returned to Copenhagen in 1829 to become ballet-master he brought with him the teachings of the French school, and he developed them in over forty ballets of his own devising. He was a highly talented choreographer and some of his creations – such as *Napoli* and his own version of *La Sylphide* – are still in the repertoire.

By a happy chance Copenhagen remained cut off from the romantic reforms at the end of the nineteenth century and preserved the old tradition; the light, quick, clean, bouncy style of the Danes seems a pure reflection of Auguste Vestris' own dancing, and the emphasis on the men is a true legacy of the eighteenth century. At the same time the company's isolation led to a falling-off of creative pressure. Dancing standards were well maintained under directors like Hans Beck at the turn of the century; but it was not until 1925 that Fokine, and five years later Balanchine, were invited to contribute to the repertoire and so enlarge its range.

Since then a progressive policy has been pursued by successive directors

Karen Kain and Sergiu Stefanschi of the National Ballet of Canada in a *pas de deux*, from John Neumeier's 'Don Juan', while the Don (Nureyev) looks on

such as Haraald Lander and Fleming Flindt (the current director). The repertoire is broad, but still built round a core of Bournonville's ballets which reveal the Danish style at its best. The merits of the school have been vividly illustrated by the dancer Erik Bruhn, who appeared as a guest star in many countries, especially in America, where his classical nobility and disciplined elegance provided a distinguished echo of European court tradition.

Partly owing to geography, the Royal Swedish Ballet has maintained links with the Danes since its foundation in 1773, by Gustavus III. In 1782 Antoine Bournonville (who married a Swede) was engaged as leading dancer and he was followed by a series of French and Italian directors: it was in Stockholm that Filippo Taglioni became father, in 1804, to a little girl called Marie. But the company had its own dancers too, and one of them, Christian Johansson, later went to Russia and became an influential teacher of the St Petersburg company.

In 1913 Fokine, who had just quarrelled with Diaghilev, arrived in Sweden with his wife and mounted many of his own ballets – an event which was to fire a local enthusiast to set up a company to rival the Ballets Russes – the Ballets Suédois, under the directorship of Rolf de Maré. The idea was to imitate Diaghilev's formula by offering programmes in which *avant-garde* experiments would alternate with dances with a national flavour. It opened in Paris in 1920 and appeared all over Europe and America, introducing some striking new works – de Maré was a genuine connoisseur with art contacts which outstripped even Diaghilev's. But the Swedish flavour proved no substitute for Russian folklore and the chief dancer and choreographer Jean Borlin was no rival to Fokine. After five years the company disbanded.

After World War I the Royal Swedish Ballet was much influenced by modern dance, and it did not return to the classical style until 1953. Since then the company has mounted most of the old classics, besides many new ballets by choreographers such as Balanchine and Tudor. The modern tradition is carried on by smaller companies, notably that of Birgit Cullberg, which has toured in America, Britain and France. There is also a large classical group in Göteborg.

If the Italians spread the fashion for classical ballet in the seventeenth century, the French in the eighteenth and nineteenth and the Russians at the start of the twentieth, it was the British who propagated it worldwide after World War II. The classical style was restored to the Vienna company in 1954 by Gavin Hamilton: the Swedish company had the same experience in 1953 with Mary Skeaping: John Cranko and Kenneth Macmillan took the classical idiom back to Stuttgart and West Berlin: South Africa has several companies led by London-trained dancers: and two British dominions, Australia and Canada, have developed ambitious companies with strong British connections.

In Australia the ground was already prepared. Small touring troupes had appeared there since the middle of the nineteenth century and in 1942 a Czech dancer, Edouard Borovansky (formerly a member of the Ballets Russes de Monte Carlo) founded a company in Melbourne which grew large enough to stage the full-length classics. It was disbanded in 1960, and in 1962 a new company, the Australian Ballet, emerged, with the British dancer, Peggy van Praagh, as director. Since then the company has grown steadily, with star

The dramatic sexual climax of Maurice Béjart's ballet to Stravinsky's 'Le Sacre du Printemps' (first choreographed by Nijinsky in 1913), with dancers of his Ballet of the Twentieth Century

Opposite above: Anjer Licher and Gérard Lemaître in Glen Tetley's 'Mutations', for the Nederlands Dans Theater, 1970

Opposite below: a scene from Rudi van Dantzig's 'Monument for a Dead Boy', for his Dutch National Ballet, 1965

guests appearing from time to time but giving way more and more to Australian dancers trained in the school, which was opened in 1964. The Australian Ballet has appeared successfully in America, Britain, France, Russia and Poland; its last director was Sir Robert Helpmann, former star dancer and choreographer with the Sadler's Wells Ballet, who has been succeeded by Anne Woolliams, a British dancer formerly attached to the Stuttgart company. There is also a smaller company in Melbourne, the Victorian Ballet Guild, and a dance company in New South Wales.

The Canadian National Ballet was founded in 1951, under the directorship of Celia Franca, formerly a dancer in the Royal Ballet company. Launched in Montreal, it found a home in Toronto, where it has quickly developed into a large and important company and school, with a repertoire mainly based on works from the Royal Ballet programme and including the nineteenth century classics. Erik Bruhn is an assistant artistic adviser. The company has toured in America, Russia, France and Britain and has mounted three seasons in New York with Nureyev as guest. Its present director is Alexander Grant, formerly of the British Royal Ballet.

The Royal Winnipeg Ballet is even older. It was founded in 1939 and has also put on the traditional classics, but emphasizes its national background in the rest of its repertoire. It has also made extensive tours, including Russia, Paris, London and Czechoslovakia. Les Grands Ballets Canadiens, a smaller and more modern troupe, is based on Montreal.

Somewhat incongruously the old traditions of nineteenth century ballet are preserved more enthusiastically than anywhere in communist countries. Poland has always been celebrated for its dancers – Nijinsky came from a Polish family – and it has a long, though interrupted, ballet history going back to the eighteenth century. Its ballet masters and teachers have included Filippo Taglioni – who mounted the full Romantic repertoire – and Cecchetti, and in more recent years former Diaghilev dancers like Leon Woizikovski and Bronislava Nijinska (the great dancer's choreographer sister) helped to put on more modern programmes. There is also a Mime Company specializing in a kind of athletic eroticism which has proved very popular abroad.

Czechoslovakia too has a ballet past – it was a famous centre in the eighteenth and nineteenth centuries – and still supports a large classical company. The Budapest Ballet in Hungary is over a hundred years old and maintains a high standard of dancing. In 1948 Vasily Vainonen, choreographer in Leningrad and Moscow, became its director and it has mounted many works from the Bolshoi repertoire. Companies in Belgrade and Bucharest are also strongly influenced by Soviet training, which can be traced as far away as Cuba – where the company is run by the internationally admired Alicia Alonso. East Berlin has also proved a fine showplace for artists from Moscow and Leningrad. In all these countries folk-dance troupes are strongly encouraged. Perhaps surprisingly, dance in Egypt is also Soviet-orientated, as for many years Soviet teachers were engaged in Cairo.

By contrast Turkish Ballet is linked to Britain. In 1947 de Valois was invited to advise on the setting up of a school, and two years later a company was founded, with a succession of members of the Royal Ballet as dancers and directors. The direction is now Turkish and many local dancers have emerged from the school.

Israel is another country in which new ballet companies are flourishing. The Bathsheva Dance Company is (like the London Contemporary Dance Theatre) an outpost of the Graham company in America and was founded in 1964 in Tel-Aviv. The Bat Dor Dance Company, founded four years later, is more classically orientated, while Inbal is primarily a folk-dance troupe.

Switzerland also supports several classical companies, of which the most prominent is at Geneva. It has strong connections with Balanchine and numbers many of his works in its repertoire. There are also classical troupes attached to the Opera Houses in Zurich, Basle and Lausanne. Portugal has a small modern troupe, the Gulbenkian Ballet, with an eclectic repertoire. Curiously, Spain has never produced a major classical company though it has a superb tradition of popular dancing and has boasted performers like the Espinosa family, Escudero, La Argentina, and in recent years, Antonio, who formed a flamenco troupe – at first with his cousin Rosario – and toured with huge success. Several other groups have followed his example.

To mention all the ballet companies in the world would be impossible; they stretch from Capetown to Reykjavik, from Tokyo to Buenos Aires. They form a network whose threads run backwards and forwards in time and cross and connect across the seas. Its members form a brotherhood in which differences of race, language and creed disappear in a single enthusiasm – the belief that dance is one of the most potent, enjoyable and rewarding activities in which any human can, in any way, partake.

XIX Les Monstres Sacrés

It has been said that there is no such thing as art – only artists. It is even truer to say that there is no such thing as dance, only dancers. In the long run ballet consists simply of a confrontation between individual performers and the audience. So it is small wonder that, in spite of efforts by directors and choreographers to suppress them, (each very naturally intent on maintaining or enlarging their own roles), stars of the dance keep emerging. There is a natural human instinct to concentrate and simplify, and in the theatre this leads to combining many loyalties and emotions within a few personalities. There is a star-shaped hole in everybody's heart, and when the right figure appears she, or he, will inevitably drop into it.

This is a lucky phenomenon for the managements. Unless a troupe is small enough to acquire an individual image, it is more effective to promote a few members of it; and from the audience's point of view it is most satisfying to fix on a single target and make it the symbolic recipient of a multitude of admiration and affection.

The story of ballet shows a long list of dancers who have filled the role in their own time – honourable names which include some of the finest artists in history. But now and then an exceptional personality emerges – a performer who not only embodies the virtues which are demanded of any outstanding artist, but who also has a personal charisma which transcends simple standards of quality and moves out into another level; they become not only the first among a few but the symbols of a whole fellowship of colleagues. These are the superstars whose luminosity spreads worldwide, legendary figures whose mysterious power works across the centuries, as strongly as any troupe or production, to keep their art alive.

Of course such apparitions are not confined to the dance. Every activity has its folk-heroes. But ballet – an art which for much of its short history aimed to be admired rather than to criticize or disturb – has thrown up an unusual number. One simple reason for this is the universality of the language. A Garrick or a Sarah Bernhardt could not exert their full powers beyond the limits of their own tongue; but a dancer can communicate as directly with his public in Berlin or Budapest as in Brazil.

It is significant that nowadays the only dramatic arts which create world stars are films, opera and ballet. It is not until a theatre personality has been disseminated on the screen that it acquires full status (mechanical reproduction has done the same for a few painters and sculptors). In the same way it is impossible for a dancer to rise to world stardom until she, or he, has had international exposure, either on television, film or, more potently, extensive touring. Yesterday's heroes earned their laurels over the roads and railways of Europe. Today's legends are born from a consensus of continents.

Their lives are not easy. Abandoning the security of their own tribe, they venture into foreign and often hostile territory. Like cuckoos they fly from land to land, descending among squawks of protest and alarm to present their outsize offering and then moving on. They arouse envy and outrage, adulation, imitation and resentment in almost equal proportions. Beyond the norm either by talent or temperament or both, they are outsiders in a close-knit society. They enjoy the prizes and they pay the price.

This is a healthy situation. As short-time visitors an instant impact is

The Stars take their curtain call after a performance in the Kirov Theatre in Leningrad. The curtain, by Alexander Golovin, dates from the days when the theatre was known as the Maryinsky, and the blue, white and gold auditorium is unchanged

essential and they tend to shape performances to stress their own talent. Art history as well as human instincts teach that such pressures must be resisted. But the sensible management accepts their inevitability and uses them, as the public gives thanks for them. For it is they who lift ballet out of the historian's files, who save it from the fatal virtues of fairness and academic rectitude, and who charge it with those emotions which excite as well as impress.

Such phenomena do not recur regularly. Every decade has its heroes and its heroines, but not even every generation throws up one of those strange creatures whom the French call 'monstres sacrés' or holy prodigies. It is tempting to analyse the qualities needed to fill the spiritual role and to look for affinities in the outstanding examples. Yet they vary enormously. It would seem that the first essential should be plain professional and technical excellence; yet Isadora Duncan, an undeniable star, was virtually untrained. You would think that a demonic temperament would be needed to drive the unresting career; yet Fonteyn is famous for her calm.

All the same, there are surely some essential ingredients. The first could be called personal topicality – the gift of embodying the dream of a whole generation. The second is the power of immediate theatrical projection, the capacity to communicate quickly with an audience unused to the artist's personal style and often – in the case of the mass audiences such performers attract – unfamiliar with the art of dance at all. The third is a mental alertness able to adapt rapidly to new situations (stars may not be intellectuals, but – outside, perhaps, the artifice of cinema – they are never stupid). The fourth is a physique tough enough to withstand the rigours of a roving life with incessant changes of time, diet and working and living conditions. The fifth is an egocentric emotional toughness able to stand up to sustained loneliness (they have no hope of normal domestic happiness) and repeated resistance. And the sixth – the mystery ingredient – is the magnetism of personality which, when communicated through their art, sells tickets – the gift of being somebody and having something to say.

Such people must always have existed, but we can only speculate on the big names in the ancient theatre. In Egypt dancers seem to have been simple cabaret entertainers unworthy of the historian's stylus. In classical Greece the theatre acquired new status, and the names of a few actors have come down to us; but dance-movement was only part of multimedia theatre and unlikely to promote celebrity on its own. In Rome 'pantomimics' like Bathyllus and Pylades were near to today's dance-theatre idols and roused genuine fan-worship. But apart from the erotic prodigies of Myrmidus little is known of their claims to popular adulation.

In the Middle Ages performers were either modest tumblers or, in the court revels, aristocratic personalities already famous in their own right. It was not until the seventeenth century, when academic pedantry began to codify and thus elevate technical prowess and theatres like the Paris Opéra were founded that the way became clear for the dominance of a professional performer over a large audience. Quickly a few artists became famous – dancers like Camargo and Sallé. But the first recognizable 'prodigy', armed with the full panoply of virtuosity and personal panache, appeared in 1749 when the Italian Gaetan Vestris joined the Paris Opéra.

Though he passed on a good measure of his reputation to his son Auguste (possibly more skilled as a dancer) nobody, either male or female, seems to have captured the public imagination to the same degree until the next century. By then ballet had become established and popular and a whole bevy of claimants to star status appeared. The celebrated print of the *Pas de Quatre* of 1845 shows four of them – Fanny Cerrito, Lucia Grahn, Carlotta Grisi and Marie Taglioni, who was to become the one to pass most vividly into history. Their partners, men like Saint Léon and Perrot and the young Lucien Petipa, had many admirers; but the role of the male dancer declined along with the standards of the Paris Opéra and ballet in general.

When the next superstar springs into the limelight we are in another century and another country. Diaghilev introduced from Russia a whole galaxy of stars. But among them all, as they recede into the past, two stand out with special prominence – Pavlova and Nijinsky, names which reach out (and this is the test) far beyond the specialist field, artists who have inspired many a child or teenager to devote their lives to the same calling. They were the heirs to the long European tradition of classical ballet; but new ideas were stirring in America and they threw up two artists of a completely new kind, dancers whose unfamiliar allure, joined to strong theatrical personalities, gave them a powerful impact. Isadora Duncan hit Europe like a whirlwind on her first tour in 1899 and continued to exert her spell even in the declining years before her death: and a generation later a young dancer in California, Martha Graham, started a revolution which, led by her own electrifying appearances, was to lead to a whole new school of dancing.

Since that time many gifted and beautiful dancers have appeared from many different countries. But none have quite achieved the symbolic status of the most recent stars in this constellation – Margot Fonteyn and Rudolf Nureyev. Once again these two have proved that a personality can carry a minority art into public awareness and become the receptacle of a whole assortment of visions and ideals.

Perhaps the greatest tribute to such superstars is the question we all begin to ask when we think about their careers coming to an end. Who, we demand, is to take their place? It is an unanswerable, even a foolish question. The essence of these artists is that they are different from all who went before them and from all who will come after. They are one-off phenomena – magic, irreplaceable and unique.

Auguste Vestris

The first idol of the dance was really two-headed, a father and son double act. The father was Gaetano Vestri, one of a large and slightly disreputable family from Florence. He came to Paris in 1747, and entered the opera dancing school – at the same time as his sister. He had some training in ballet and exceptional natural talent, and although he was already eighteen years old he was taken into the company the next year and was promoted to 'premier danseur' the year after, and when the current star, Dupré, retired in 1751 he succeeded him.

To begin with, Vestri – or Vestris as he now called himself – tackled character as well as 'noble' parts, but he soon specialized in the grand roles of gods and heroes. His style was eloquent and elegant at the same time, he was very handsome, and he was famous for his beautiful legs which he displayed in the dignified dances of the day. He became the rage of Paris.

But success went to his head. He became preposterously demanding and notoriously pompous. ('There are only three great men in Europe – the King of Prussia, Monsieur Voltaire and me.') A year after his promotion to principal dancer he quarrelled with another artist, drew his sword on him in the theatre and was thrown into prison. On his release he left Paris and toured Berlin and Turin; but within three years he was back at the Opéra, and later became the maître de ballet. He was a frequent guest at Stuttgart at Noverre's invitation, and later appeared with great success in London.

Though he put on airs of nobility, dancers still rated low in society at that time, and their morals did not elevate them. He had many mistresses and one of them, an attractive and promiscuous French dancer called Marie Allard, bore him a son in 1760. He was called Auguste, and was to become the first true international ballet superstar.

His path to fame was a smooth one. 'It is only natural that Auguste is more talented than I am', remarked his father, in whom arrogance seems to have outweighed jealousy. 'He has Gaetano as his father, an advantage which nature denied me.' He inherited not only the glamour of his father's name (though, since his parents were not married, Auguste was known at first as Vestr'allard) but the immense benefits of his teaching and his official influence.

His debut was sensational. During the interval of a performance in 1772 Gaetano led the twelve-year-old boy on the stage and introduced him. 'Now, my son, show the public your talents. Your father is watching you.' The little Auguste performed a chaconne with such lightness and dexterity that the audience was delighted. 'What talent!' exclaimed Dauberval, one of Gaetano's colleagues mischievously. 'And he is Vestris's son, not mine. Alas, I only missed it by a quarter of an hour!'

Critics found that he combined 'the majesty of his father with the gaiety of his mother', and the slim blond youth quickly became a star attraction, a Cupid with the heels of Mercury who also quickly took on his youthful shoulders his father's title (invented by a promotion-minded brother), 'Le Dieu de la Danse'.

He was a very different kind of ballet-god – Dionysus rather than Apollo. Small and quick with a lively jump, a vigorous acting style, and exceptionally easy beats and turns (he was famous for his pirouettes) he was no rival for his father's majestic manoeuvres; but he was perfectly designed to develop the new virtuoso elements in ballet now that it had been freed from masks and heavy conventional costumes. Noverre rated him 'the most astonishing dancer in Europe' and he made sensational guest appearances in many cities, including London, where Burke cancelled a debate in Parliament so that members might see him and his father dance.

He returned to London every year until the Revolution and was even maître de ballet for a short time at the King's Theatre; but Paris was his home. At first, encouraged by his father, he showed signs of the family arrogance and profligacy. He had his first taste of prison, after a row, at the age of thirteen; in 1782 he gave notice but was not allowed to leave France; and in 1788 he was arrested for refusing to perform for Marie Antionette before the King of Sweden.

But in the end he remained at the Opéra as *premier danseur* for thirty-six years, ending as a kindly teacher and the invaluable coach of Taglioni, Elssler and Grahn. He retired officially as a dancer at the age of fifty-six; but in 1835 he made a last appearance to dance a minuet and gavotte with Taglioni, who presented the seventy-five-year-old legend with her flowers. He had dazzled two generations with the gifts he had inherited from his father; and through his pupils Bournonville and Perrot and a long line of dancers he was to be the ancestor of countless stars to come. He died in Paris in 1842.

Auguste Vestris. Oil painting by Adèle Romance, *dite* Romany

Marie Taglioni

Marie Taglioni was – and remains – the archetypal international ballerina. Her father was Italian, her mother was Swedish and before she was ten she had lived in Stockholm, Vienna and Kassel and been smuggled in a French general's carriage into Paris. She was to make her debut in Austria and her reputation in France. Her career carried her to almost every capital in Europe. Her name on a poster sold out theatres from London to St Petersburg for twenty years. She earned ecstatic criticisms, enormous fees and a host of admirers and she died at eighty, poor and almost forgotten, 'a very old lady who had never been pretty but whose expression is still attractive', as her grandson described her.

She was trained in the French school but her real teacher was her father Filippo. She was skinny and somewhat round-shouldered as a child and was never to be a beauty; she had small, almost pinched features, a sharp nose and very long arms and legs. But he seized on her rare quality of movement, made it into an expressive instrument and arranged dances which displayed it to the full. In six performances at the Paris Opéra in 1837, at the age of twenty-three, she established herself as the eternal symbol. 'Her debut will open a new Epoch,' wrote *Le Figaro*. 'It is Romanticism applied to the dance.'

Her style was supremely summarized in a ballet which her father devised for her in 1832, *La Sylphide*. The contrast between her delicate and evasive style (glimpsed the previous year in an opera, *Robert le Diable*) and the assertive charms of her predecessors was revolutionary and she, and the ballet, became a cultural milestone as clear as Victor Hugo's play *Hernani* had been two years earlier. The Romantic Movement was launched.

Like all great stars she both represented her time and transcended it. She stood for the new ideal of womanhood. Sturdy and palpable sex-appeal, laced with acrobatics, was replaced by a vision more acceptable to the new middle-class. Purity was paramount. As immaterial as a spirit, the new heroine was frail and natural, arousing manly emotions with no danger of a real embrace. The embodiment of a naughty dream, the chaste seductress melted into the air leaving her admirers with rapturous memories and the solid comforts of domesticity.

Taglioni perfectly fitted this still unconscious demand. She was not rounded nor vivacious, but her slim figure with its demure shoulders, narrow feet and graceful neck, coupled with her trick of bending modestly forwards with her arms lowered or crossed (which concealed their length) became the model for Victorian girls.

Though skilfully exploited by her father, the manner was evidently a reflection of her real character – dutiful, dedicated and a bit prim. With her strict Franco-Italian training behind her she developed into an unsullied classical stylist without a trace of 'demi-caractère' dash, lyrical and musical. Her phrasing must have been poetic and her interpretations – though closely worked out – sensitive and exquisitely theatrical. Her very first appearance hit her audience with an explosion of modesty.

Technically, she excelled in just those qualities needed for the new heroine – lightness, smoothness, softness and poise. She was compared to a gazelle, to a cloud, to a 'shadow condensed into a mist'. She floated and skimmed and 'shimmered' (her own phrase); her point-work must have been accurate but never brilliant. She avoided all tricks and showy movements and concentrated on a simplicity which seemed the very sign of virginity.

Every report picks on her refinement and decorum. Contrasting her style with the 'sensuality' of her predecessors, the Opéra's director later wrote that her father had demanded of her 'an easy grace, lightness, fine elevation and spring; but he did not permit a gesture or a pose which offended decency and modesty. His aim was that women and young girls could watch her without blushing.' Many of her subsequent imitators turned this into a simpering gentility. But Taglioni's dancing had the ring of sincerity, of poetic sensibility. She was a goddess who was also a lady.

Fame enveloped her instantly and never left (though she had to endure some rough criticisms; even her champion Gautier was complaining after eleven years of a loss of speed and elevation). She left Paris and toured triumphantly all over Europe, finally retiring after a performance in England, where she had appeared regularly in London and the provinces, at the age of forty-three.

She had briefly married and borne a daughter and a probably illegitimate son. She had no regular partner (the brilliant Jules Perrot had proved too popular for her liking) or companion. Her considerable savings disappeared mysteriously. For thirty-two years she earned a meagre living by teaching, first in Paris and then in London and Brighton, where she instructed young ladies in deportment – a spinsterish reflection of her stage personality.

She died in 1884 in Marseilles. Her style was outmoded, but its ghost still flits like a sylph through romantic ballet, a 'sweet melancholy joy, a chaste passion', as Berlioz described it. It was to float in 1909 through *Les Sylphides* and it hovers still over the head of every young girl who dreams of soft music and herself in a white tutu.

Marie Taglioni. Lithograph by Delpech from a drawing by Z. Belliard

Fanny Elssler

'Spirituality is something to be respected, but in the dance some concessions can well be made to materialism,' wrote Théophile Gautier, who had been the first to acclaim the incorporeal Taglioni. He was disloyally celebrating a new ballerina at the Paris Opéra, Fanny Elssler. Only six years younger than the great Italian dancer, she became her immediate rival. No two dancers could have been more different, nor complemented each other better.

Elssler was born in Vienna in 1810 where her father was copyist to the composer Haydn, and was introduced at an early age into the Imperial school of dance. (Legend has it that even before then she had attended girls' classes with a doubtful reputation.) A precocious little beauty, she quickly attracted attention. At twelve she was in the opera *corps de ballet* watching Taglioni make her debut; at thirteen she was doing a *pas de deux*; and at seventeen she was sent to air her charms in Naples, which she did so successfully that she returned pregnant by the King's brother.

Back in Vienna, she took on leading roles and an affair with an elderly political writer. A tour in Germany sparked off a romance with her partner and established her as a powerful actress who could not only turn on tears on stage, but extract them from the audience, while her gaiety could light up the whole theatre. Her youth, pretty face and vitality were captivating, and she had a natural contact with the public. Indeed after her debut in London at the age of twenty-three one critic remarked that 'she would be more successful if her appeals to the audience were not quite so frequent.'

In England she survived comparison with Taglioni, but her real test was to be in Paris. Her ardent temperament was shrewdly publicized in advance; a rumour was even put about that she had had an affair in Vienna with the ill-starred son of Napoleon, the Duc de Reichstadt. Her charms were advertised as 'great vivacity, astonishing strength, precision emerging from apparent carelessness . . . movement of eye and head which are particularly enticing. Add to that a pretty face, ravishing shoulders, fine arms, perfect legs and feet and one can forecast a mad success.'

She was evidently a demi-caractère dancer with enormous sex-appeal. In September 1834, after some extra coaching by the aged Auguste Vestris, she made her Paris debut as a fairy in a mediocre ballet based on Shakespeare's *The Tempest*. Her triumph was instantaneous. Her accurate and lively dancing, her voluptuous personality, vivid mime and roguish charm conquered all. 'She was not like Taglioni, a sylphide or a daughter of the skies,' wrote a contemporary. 'She came down to earth and her looks inspired men with hopes which were more positive.'

But her biggest success was to come. Two years later, in *Le Diable Boîteux*, a dramatic ballet packed with Spanish local colour (much in vogue in Paris at the time) she arranged for herself a castanet-clicking number called *La Cachucha* which brought the house down and became the rage of Europe. The critics were transported. 'How she twists! How she bends! What fire! What voluptuousness!'

Her stage personality was fixed, vivacious, intelligent and dramatic, with an attraction which sometimes transcended her sex. 'Now she is the most charming girl, now she is the most charming boy,' wrote Gautier of her. 'She is Hermaphrodite, able to separate at will the two beauties which are blended in her.' We are far from Taglioni's frail femininity.

After wild successes in Vienna and London (where she acquired a new lover) she took a revolutionary decision. She set off to conquer an unknown country – America. In May 1840 she stepped into New York and a few days later opened at the Park Theatre. The *corps de ballet* consisted only of sixteen 'miserable sticks' but her 'Cracovienne' from *The Gypsy* won her an ovation. Soon she had set off on one of those tours round which countless dancers were to follow her – Philadelphia, Washington, Baltimore and Boston. After a return to New York and a brief stop-off at Havana, she returned home, well satisfied. In under two years she had done 200 performances and earned a fortune.

Trouble awaited her in Paris, where the Opéra sued her (successfully) for breach of contract. For seven years she toured the capitals of Europe, through Germany, Austria, England, Belgium, Hungary – even Ireland. She danced *Giselle* giving new and decisive stress to the dramatic Act I, and found new scope for her wit and tragedy in *Esmeralda*. In 1848 anti-Austrian feeling drove her out of Italy and she turned up – without a contract – in St Petersburg.

At first there was hesitation. But her *Esmeralda* clinched her success, leaving a heritage of expressive movement which is alive today. The Tsar gave her lessons in rifle-drill. She danced with the young Marius Petipa, and appeared in his first Russian production. She conquered Moscow. She was forty-one and had the ballet world at her feet.

She returned to Vienna and announced her retirement, withdrawing to the country where (like Taglioni she lived on for over thirty years). She had contributed much. 'Mlle Taglioni is a Christian dancer and Mlle Elssler is a pagan dancer,' Gautier had written. Ballet has room for both.

Fanny Elssler. Oil painting, artist unknown

Isadora Duncan

Elssler's pioneering in America left a permanent legacy of classical ballet. But Isadora Duncan, the greatest dancing star to come out of America, did not snatch up the torch carried over from Europe; she flung it in the faces of its worshippers and marched forwards with a strange bright flame of her own.

Duncan was born in San Francisco in 1878. Her father was an eccentric newspaper man of Irish stock who had to flee from the police and deserted his family. His wife gave piano lessons for a living and these led to dancing in the parlour and, eventually, to dancing lessons conducted by little Isadora and her sister. The whole family was stage-struck and moved to Chicago where Isadora joined a mime company which took her to New York and then to London, where she briefly took ballet classes with an ex-pupil of Elssler. But she was a girl with a strong sense of mission and soon she was back in New York displaying her art-nouveau style poses and movements in society salons. Encouraged by some success, she set out to conquer London.

She had the luck to get some recitals in an art gallery and then moved on to Paris, where society again welcomed her; after a few months she was in Berlin with a rather dubious troupe run by Loie Fuller. Slowly, her fame expanded. Classical ballet had become a huge fossilized spectacle and here was something new. Her simple emotional movements, daring presentation (bare arms and legs and see-through costumes) and potent feminine charm were like a refreshing shower.

Her dances were controlled improvisations – interpretations of music she chose herself from her favourite composers; she designed her own simple costumes and settings; and she danced alone (later she had a few young girls to support her). She was a dancing ego – and in this she was the equivalent of the cabaret singers of her time rather than of any ballet star. But she brought personality-exploitation into the service of serious art. She despised and denounced the gymnastics of classical ballet. And she ignored the musical-box scores which served them. In all this she led the way to the reforms of the next generation.

Photographs of her in her youth show a pretty face and she was described at that time as 'graceful and slender'. But the strain of drawing her whole inspiration out of her own personality taxed her severely. Her love of artistic freedom began to overflow into her private life. She was taken up by fashionable society, and champagne began to bolster her hard-taxed energies. She became as famous for her sexual generosity as for her art, going through a long rota of lovers of whom the most famous was the stage designer Gordon Craig. An exotic and extravagant nomad, she toured from capital to capital across Europe.

In 1905 she paid her first visit to Russia. Here too change was in the air, and she rode in triumph on the current which was bringing in the new ideas of Stanislavsky and the artists of the *Mir Iskusstva*. She was fêted by the aristocracy and admired by (and admired) the twenty-five-year-old Fokine and even the more conservative Pavlova.

On her return to Paris she failed to compete with Diaghilev's first concerts. She returned to America – disastrously until she was given engagements by the conductor of the New York Philharmonic orchestra. Back in Paris she was again unsuccessful, coinciding this time with Diaghilev's first ballet season. But the situation was saved by the millionaire son of Isaac Singer, the man who had invented the sewing-machine. He became her lover, showered her with presents and took her away on his yacht. He even financed a Duncan school in Paris.

But the shadows were closing in. In 1913 tragedy struck, when her two children (one by Craig, the other by Singer) were drowned when a taxi ran backwards into the Seine. The outbreak of war further shattered her plans, and she lost another baby by a chance acquaintance. But she gallantly battled on. In 1921 she was dancing in London a number extolling the Russian Revolution. A Soviet commissar saw her and she was invited to found a school in the new Russia.

The visit was a huge personal success, and lit a flame in the breast of a wild young poet half her age, Sergei Essenin. In a delirium of happiness they were married, and she took him off on a tour of America. It turned into a tragic-comic disaster, with drink and temperament flowing. He left her and, later, committed suicide. Duncan returned to France but by now she was an over-substantial shadow of her former self. With no basic training behind her, her powers declined and she was sheltering, penniless and lonely, in the South of France when she was killed in a motor accident in 1927.

She was forty-nine and by now a battered legend. A self-expressionist from first to last, it is hard to separate her art from her personality. By renouncing classical technique she put herself outside academic criticism, but it is clear that she had superbly expressive plasticity and a sense of musical phrasing which gave the simplest movement beauty and feeling. She also had a strong stage personality and total conviction in her work. In her approach she was a child of the nineteenth century (she detested films and jazz and saw herself as a Priestess of Art). She was immature, egocentric and often absurd. But professionals like Duse and Fokine admired her as much as uncritical worshippers. Like all stars, she convinced those who saw her that behind her dancing lay a true element of greatness.

Isadora Duncan. Photographed by Arnold Genthe

Anna Pavlova

If Isadora Duncan carried to some excess the 'material' charms which Gautier had found so irresistible in Elssler, the balance towards spirituality was to be devastatingly restored. Simultaneously the untrained inspirations of the girl from California were countered by an artist springing from the very heart of professional ballet – Anna Pavlova.

Pavlova won her extraordinary fame not through any originality or idiosyncracy, but through sheer quality. She was not an outsider but the peer of a whole army of accomplished colleagues. Dedicated and single-minded she carried tradition to a peak where it blended with personal inspiration to produce an image which became the symbol of her whole art.

She was born in St Petersburg in 1881, the only daughter of a laundry-woman. Her father was probably a Jewish financier called Lazar Poliakov. She was a frail but determined little girl who made up her mind to become a prima ballerina. She left home and, at ten, enrolled in the Ballet School.

From the first her exceptional talent was obvious but she slogged through the full eight years' course, acquiring a strength which – added to her natural delicacy – was to be the foundation of a long career of unparalleled intensity. She entered the Maryinsky company at eighteen and almost at once took over solo roles. With the help of extra coaching – probably paid for by her real father – she made such progress that in her third season she was given the ballerina role in *Giselle*.

In an age of virtuous ballerinas her tender grace was an echo of the old style. 'She reminds us of some long-past romantic days,' wrote an elderly admirer. 'She looks like Taglioni.'

But she was not all modest obedience. In 1905 she took part in a strike and she sucked in new and unorthodox ideas from her old fellow-pupil, Fokine. After Duncan's Russian visit he arranged a plastic-style Greek ballet for her, and the next year he gave her the romantic *pas de deux* in a piece evoking the old days, *Chopiniana*, later to be remodelled as *Les Sylphides*. In the same year he arranged a solo for her to Saint-Saëns's *Dying Swan*. Written in a few minutes, this slight and very Duncanesque piece – all emotional simplicity – was to become the most celebrated of all her interpretations.

Perhaps made restless by Fokine's new ideas, she embarked in 1908 on a tour of Europe's northern capitals. Diaghilev was launching his Ballets Russes in the West, and next year she was in Prague, Berlin and Vienna, before joining him for the later part of his sensational first season in Paris. She was received with rapture but did not eclipse Karsavina and Nijinsky who were already established as favourites. She did not agree to appear with him the following year, especially when she heard the score of *The Firebird* which had been planned for her.

Instead she sailed to America, where she appeared in *Coppélia* at the Metropolitan Opera House in New York before setting out on a tour which took her to the West Coast. From there she travelled to London, where she appeared at the head of her own company, starting an enterprise which was to embrace her whole career. She made two more brief appearances with Diaghilev; but henceforward she was to prefer touring with her own troupe,

with a house in London as her centre.

In this policy, as in all else, she carried the concept of the international superstar to extremes. A compulsive performer by temperament, she adopted a personal mission to carry her art to audiences in remote corners of the globe. She returned several times to Russia and was a regular visitor to Europe. But she also penetrated regions hitherto unfamiliar with ballet. After spending the years of the 1914 war in North and South America, she toured Egypt, India, Shanghai and Japan. In 1925 she was in South Africa, Australia and New Zealand, and in 1929 she visited Burma, Singapore and Java. A burning missionary of the dance who did not flinch at village halls, sordid hotels and three performances a day on primitive stages. She wore herself out with overwork, and died in The Hague, aged forty-nine, at the start of a new season.

Obliviously self-centred – partners, conductors and supporting dancers had to yield to her demands and she preferred unobtrusive music and designs – she was as unsparing of others as she was of herself. Narrow in her interests and old-fashioned in her tastes, jealous, and puritanically domineering (though she had several affairs and seems not to have married the man who ran her company and shared her London home), she preserved a childlike emotional and intellectual simplicity which protected her sensitive theatrical gift – a dance quality which has never been surpassed, with an innate stage glamour and a sincerity which lit up her slightest diversion. She was, like Taglioni, exceptionally slender yet strong, and she had the same ethereal, lyrical grace. But to this she added a dark, exotic (perhaps Jewish) streak which gave depth to her acting, and also a fire and speed which could turn her into the essence of vitality and gaiety. The spirits of a long line of dancers seem to have united to make her the last, and perhaps the greatest, of the old-time ballerinas.

Vaslav Nijinsky

The premiere of Diaghilev's Ballets Russes in Paris in 1909 announced a new age in ballet, and it was symbolized by the arrival of a new kind of star. The top artist of that season was Pavlova, the exquisite fruit of a tradition of which France itself had been the cradle; but the novelty-hungry public fastened even more eagerly on a dancer who offered undreamed-of sensations – Vaslav Nijinsky. Though they danced together in the West only a few times, their names have been linked ever since in legend. In this visionary partnership Pavlova is the heiress to the nineteenth century; Nijinsky, though he was visibly a product of the Symbolist movement, is a portent of our own age.

He had, in fact, emerged from the professional ballet establishment in the same way as she had. Born in Kiev in 1889 to Polish dancer parents, he entered the St Petersburg ballet school in 1898. He was quickly recognized as a prodigy, though sombre by temperament and slow at book-learning. He completed the full eight years' training, graduated dazzlingly, and was taken into the Maryinsky company at the age of eighteen with a brilliant future before him.

It was not to take the conventional course, which might have brought him national fame, but not international glory. He was immediately taken up by the rich, permissive St Petersburg set and spotted by Diaghilev, who became his admirer and lover and invited him to star in his first season in Paris. With this inspired patron to present and promote him, a brilliant company to back him and – most important – a choreographer of genius, Fokine, to develop and display his particular gifts, he could be counted the luckiest of artists; and in fact, within a few short seasons, he became a celebrity. In a series of short works which Fokine arranged for him – *Le Spectre de la Rose, Schéhérazade, Petrushka* – he created an image which was both drenched in his period and which helped to form its style.

But, as in the story of *The Sleeping Beauty*, one fatal gift was added to the blessings which attended his debut; like Aurora he was to fall into oblivion at the height of his success, a sleep from which no Prince Charming could wake him. His elder brother had been committed to an asylum as a child and Vaslav had a share of instability. The strains of his profession were increased when, after a quarrel with the management of the Maryinsky Theatre, to which he had returned regularly between his seasons with Diaghilev, he was dismissed. From then on he was committed to the nomadic career of an international star.

He found himself under extra pressure through embarking – with great originality – on choreography of his own (*L'Après-midi d'un Faune, Le Sacre du Printemps, Jeux*) and in 1913, while on the boat taking the company on its first tour outside Europe, to South America, he suddenly proposed to a young society lady, married her and found himself dismissed. His creative relationship with Diaghilev was severed.

Following in Pavlova's footsteps he accepted an invitation to appear with his own company at a London music-hall. But this time the declaration of independence was not a success. World War I broke out and he was trapped in Hungary for two years, after which he briefly joined Diaghilev again in New York. But all artistic intimacy was broken with the personal one. Diaghilev returned to Europe, while Nijinsky led the company on a troubled five-month tour round the states (creating on the way one more ballet, *Tyl Eulenspiegel*). He made one more trip to South America with the Ballets Russes where, in October 1917, he danced for the last time. He was twenty-eight.

Back in Switzerland he developed eccentric symptons, and he lapsed slowly into insanity. His career – a mere ten years – was over but, as Taglioni and Elssler had done, he lived on for thirty years after his retirement. He died in London in 1950.

His career had been a phenomenon to which this tragic ending added a final touch of melodrama. He had created a completely new genre of dancer. In place of the noble and powerful partners of the nineteenth century he presented an exotic and narcissistic little figure (he was only 5 ft 4 in), remote, ambiguous, erotic rather than romantic. His technique was clearly formidable, based on an exceptional high, soft jump; but neither his convoluted style, his short thick figure nor his intersex personality fitted him to be a classical dancer in the old style. Instead he created a category of his own, excelling in half-human chimeras – fauns, birds, dolls, spirits.

Off-stage he was unobtrusive to the point of dimness and inarticulate to the point of dumbness; but as soon as he had his make-up on some barrier was lifted and he changed into a burning theatrical personality whose hang-ups were translated into magnetic mystery and whose physical idiosyncracies became new aspects of beauty. His unique plasticity could surely have been adapted to today's dance-style, but he was not given the chance. For a few short seasons he flashed across the ballet stage; then he leaped into the darkness of legend.

Vaslav Nijinsky in 'Giselle'

Martha Graham

As though only half-satisfied with Isadora Duncan, America was to produce – less than a generation later – another revolutionary of the dance who was to become one of its idols – Martha Graham. She was born in 1894 in Chicago but, like Duncan, she grew up in California, where as a child she saw the pioneer couple Ted Shawn and Ruth St Denis. She was fired with the desire to dance and joined their troupe, performing ethnic roles – Egyptian, Mexican, Oriental – in the art nouveau style of the period.

Soon she was in New York appearing (again like Duncan) in a commercial show, and there she formed her own group (all girls, like Duncan's) for which she arranged the dances herself. Slowly she developed an individual style and a system of training to achieve it. At first she was much influenced by her music director, Louis Horst (who was familiar with Central European dancers); but later she took on (and married) a male ballet dancer. Her work became freer and lighter and she began to introduce into her work the tension between the sexes which had so far been missing.

This did not flower into the sentimental idyll of classical ballet. She was fanatically serious and wedded to the primitivism preached by Shawn and St Denis, and in her ballets the attraction between the hero and the heroine (invariably herself) was sexual rather than romantic. She explored primeval emotions and deep psychological waters in strong barefoot movements which were appropriately earth-bound and physical, in place of the spiritual soaring and graceful floating of classical ballet.

At first she was appreciated by only a small group – not the society ladies who had taken up dance as a fad, but earnest students and disciples. Conventional audiences were shaken by her angular movements (related to futurist developments in art), her expressionist emoting and her severe avoidance of spectacle and charm. But slowly she drove a wedge into the delicate flank of the classical dance and finally emerged as a recognized American pioneer, with government-sponsored tours and massive recognition abroad.

Through her originality and her unprecedented length of career (fifty years of dancing, as opposed to thirty by Duncan and only ten by Nijinsky) she has been both the fount and the focus of the whole non-classical dance movement in America, throwing off creative splinter groups, as her dancers, following her own precepts, deserted her to develop their own trends. Her foreign tours mostly came late in her career when her dance capacities were fading. But her dark, exotic appearance and personality, and the concentrated force of her highly emotional acting were still overwhelming, while the impact of her company in her stark dramas, rich with symbols, everywhere overcame initial resistance.

Surviving two world wars and a depression with indomitable tenacity, she toured the United States indefatigably and became a well-known national figure; and journeys to South America, Europe, Israel, India and the Far East raised her to international celebrity – never a big box-office draw but everywhere a controversial force of major impact inspiring bands of devotees and disciples.

Graham was both the creator of her company and its director; she was its choreographer, teacher and performing star. It was simply an extension of her own personality. This was complex and contradictory, a combination in which an aggressively rebellious drive was blended with high-minded missionary zeal, a daughter of the revolution in the role of priestess. To this she added a generous touch of theatrical glamour. Her love of independence and individual free expression is typical of her American pioneer background. But at the centre of every activity was a star stage personality which carried her ideas – which inevitably became old-fashioned – across the decades, and enabled her to marry Symbolist mysticism with Freudian psychology. We can trace the progress of her career as a dancer in the ballets she created, from charming period divertissements to sex-charged struggles in a tangle of phallic symbols and finally doom-laden epics in which the heroine finally yields in anguish to forces stronger than herself. She gave up performing at the age of seventy-nine.

Graham's influence has been exerted not only through her own performances, but through those of her disciples. This was made possible by her unique gifts as a teacher; unlike Duncan she worked out a rational system which could codify and so perpetuate the disciplines of her dancing. She was a mixture of Salome, Elektra and Old Testament prophet, who brought her own handwritten tablets down from the mountain and passed them on for future generations to follow.

Martha Graham in 'Deaths and Entrances'. Photographed by Chris Alexander

Margot Fonteyn

Every age has its own ideals and heroines. Margot Fonteyn may be the heiress to a long tradition; but she was born in this century and her career has been very different from those of her famous forbears – no fierce dedication nor stormy struggles, but a long, smooth determined curve. As though wafted in the arms of fortune she seems to have floated to the top with a smoothness as effortless as her dancing.

Of course her success has actually been as hard-earned as the seamless fluency of her movement. She has risen to fame the hard way – straight up the centre path of tradition. Luck has played a part, as it does in the history of all stars – the luck to be born at the right time in the right place with the right qualities. But she has added to her rare gifts exceptional qualities of character – intelligence, charm and a streak of ruthlessness which expresses itself in single-minded concentration and self-discipline.

She was born in Surrey in 1919 (real name Peggy Hookham) and slipped into ballet almost by accident. She was never stage-struck but just proceeded with exceptional facility from one to another of the dancing schools to which her half-Brazilian mother sent her, starting in Ealing at the age of four. Her engineer father was often sent abroad and she later found herself in Hong Kong and Shanghai where, aged eleven, she studied under an ex-Maryinsky teacher. Two years later she was back in London with an old Russian ballerina and it was here that Ninette de Valois was invited by Mrs Hookham to see her.

Immediately impressed by the dark little girl with her impish, rather oriental features, de Valois took her on as a pupil in her new Sadlers Wells School. The very same year she made her stage debut as a Snowflake in *The Nutcracker*. She was fifteen. Within a year she was taking leading roles in new ballets and even danced Odette in *Swan Lake* (the virtuoso part of Odile being taken by an older dancer). With the disappearance from the company of Markova in 1936 to start her own troupe, Fonteyn became the star of the five-year-old company.

She had learned much by watching Markova but was very different both physically and temperamentally. Fortunately, Frederick Ashton, the young choreographer who was to create most of the company's new repertoire over the next twenty years understood her special qualities, as Fokine had understood Nijinsky's, saw that they matched his own style and developed them by making her the vehicle of his gentle English lyricism. In a whole series of ballets he brought out her tender sincerity, quiet wit and soft classical correctness. In a work like *Symphonic Variations* her lack of affectation became an almost bravura hallmark.

Though her style appeared most openly in roles specially written for her, it was in the nineteenth-century classics that she showed her true mettle. Born with an ideal physique for dancing, slim and supple, with a small dark head, huge eyes and delicately elegant legs and arms, she had a fluency, grace and harmony of line which made difficult steps look easy and could translate an acrobatic feat into an expressive gesture. Like all great stars, she had the capacity to harness her own personality. Her cool well-organized equanimity (she is an excellent committee woman) became on stage the serene authority which is the essence of the classical style. But her femininity brought warmth and feeling to the most abstract movement, while her sense of timing and musicality, plus a theatrical instinct which was born partly from a quick intelligence, added the essential touch of stage magic.

It was in the great ballerina role in *The Sleeping Beauty* that she conquered New York when the company first appeared there in 1949. By then she had established herself as the undisputed star of British ballet. She was thirty and it seemed that she had reached her peak. In 1955 she married the ambassador from Panama and in the next few years she seemed to be destined for a gradual retirement. But the sudden arrival in the West of a young Russian dancer nearly twenty years her junior gave a late and unexpected impetus to her career, extended it into an incredible final lap and carried her to world stardom.

In 1962 she appeared with Rudolf Nureyev for the first time at Covent Garden, in *Giselle* – a role in which she had, curiously, never excelled. At once it was clear that a rare partnership had been born. Her radiant Apollonian calm was perfectly offset by his Dionysiac passion, and the artistic sympathy between them brought out untapped qualities which carried her triumphantly from capital to capital, in an unparalleled autumn of success. She had never been a virtuoso performer, and her true qualities shone brighter than ever, a luminous example of restraint carried to triumphant success.

Margot Fonteyn in 'Swan Lake'. Photographed by Houston Rogers

XX The Theoreticians

Because dance is by its nature a purely physical phenomenon, not much public attention is given to the cerebral activities behind the presentations in the theatre. Commentaries had apparently been composed since the earliest times, but the essay written in the second century by Lucian (if it was by him – his disregard for dance elsewhere raises suspicions) is apparently the first to survive, though Quintilian had recommended dancing – presumably in its Roman mime form – for would-be orators even earlier. The real ancestor of academic theoreticians was an Italian dancing-master of the fifteenth century, Domenico de Piacenza.

One of the 101 plates by J. G. Puschner in Gregorio Lambranzi's *Neue und Curieuse Theatralische Tantz-Schule*, published in Nuremberg in 1716. Each illustration is accompanied by instructions and the appropriate music

He seems to have been a man of some distinction, attached to the court of Lionello Sforza in Ferrara. About 1416 he wrote a treatise called *De Arte Saltandi et Choreos Ducendi* ('Art of Performing and Arranging Dances'). He set out clearly a list of the virtues admired in dancers of his time; they were much the same as now – grace, agility, control and a fluent manner of rising and dipping 'like a gondola on the waves'. He also made a distinction between different types of dance – the basic *danza* and the more varied *ballo* – and drew up twelve movements – nine 'natural' and three 'artificial' such as flourishes, glides and pirouettes, which he thought unsuitable for ladies. At the same time he listed four sorts of dance – the *bassa danza*, the *quadrerna*, the *saltarello* and the *piva* – and proceeded to set down some examples of them, fifteen *balli* and five *danze*.

He had a pupil who wrote even more fully, Guglielmo Ebreo (William the Jew), whose *De Practica seu Arte Tripudii* of 1463 has come down to us in several manuscripts. He was a ballet-master who worked both in his native Pesaro and in Milan, Mantua, Naples and Venice and he became a colleague of Domenico in Ferrara. He provided a charming definition of dance:

An action which shows outwardly the movements of the spirit which, in accordance with the measures and perfect concords of harmony descend with earthly joy through our hearing into our mind, and there produce sweet movements which, being thus imprisoned as it were in defiance of nature, endeavour to escape and reveal themselves.

He also furnished a list of the qualities of the good dancer – *mesura* (rhythm), *partira del terreno* (a sense of space), *aierel* (grace and lightness), *memoria* (memory), *maniera* (style) as well as *movimento corporeo* (plasticity) and *mistico* (mood). He instructed the girls to keep their heads up and their eyes down and, at the end of the dance when her partner leaves her, the girl should 'face him squarely, with a sweet regard, and make a decent and respectful curtsey in answer to his bow'. He provided a set of seventeen dance tunes (one of them by no less a personage than Lorenzo the Magnificent), and intricate instructions for figures by various couples. He even advocated practising rhythm by dancing against the beat. Another pupil of Domenico, Antonio Cornazano, a well-born poet and essayist who was born in Piacenza, published in 1465 a book called *Il Libro dell' arte del Danzare* elaborating the same principles. He was not always very explicit, remarking 'This cannot be well explained unless you are there to be made to do it'; but, like another writer of the same period, Ambrosio de Pesaro, he refined Domenico's

Above: Jean-Georges Noverre, 1727–1810, dancer, choreographer and author of *Lettres sur la Danse* (1760), which opened the way to all later developments of theatrical dance. Engraving by Barthélemy Roger after a drawing by Guérin

Opposite: a page from Raoul Feuillet's *Choréographie ou l'Art de Décrire la Danse*, 1699. In this early attempt at dance-notation the emphasis was laid on the floor patterns; the normally acceptable steps were conventional and limited

teaching in a period when ballets were very much in fashion.

In 1588, Jehan Tabouret, canon of Langres, published under the pseudonym of Thoinot Arbeau a detailed description of the dances of his day with the title *Orchésographie*.

But it was the eighteenth century, the age of reason, which saw the real foundations of a dance aesthetic. In 1678 a Dutch philologist called Van Meursius solemnly catalogued dozens of (supposed) antique dances from Greece and Rome; in 1712 John Weaver published in London his *Essay towards a History of Dancing*, advocating 'scenical dancing', that is a balanced blend of form and content, and complaining of 'too much capering and tumbling'; and in 1716 a Venetian, Gregorio Lambranzi, brought out a guide for dance teachers, *Nuova e curiosa Scuola de' Balli*. Later in the century, in the *Encyclopédie* of 1772, Diderot, evidently a keen follower of ballet, devoted nearly ten full pages to it with a history going back to Moses celebrating the crossing of the Red Sea and ending with the Dance of St Vitus. He wrote prophetically:

It is probable that one day, without changing the music – which is impossible – the whole constitution of the Italian opera will be altered and it will take on the natural and piquant form of a French ballet.

He foresaw theatrical magic, rather than tragedy or comedy, as its proper sphere. But the most important treatise on dance to date – and one of the most crucial of all time – was published in Germany in 1760 by a Frenchman – Jean-Georges Noverre's *Lettres sur la Danse*, a long, detailed and original work putting forward a number of reforms.

Like almost all reformers, he demanded a 'return to nature'. 'Poetry, painting and drawing, Sir, are or should be no other than a faithful likeness of beautiful nature' he declared, and went on surprisingly: 'It is owing to the accuracy of representation that the works of men like Corneille and Racine, Raphael and Michelangelo have been handed down to posterity'. He raised his voice (a generation before the painter David) against the artificiality of rococo. He advocated a closer attention to plot and period, less exaggeration in the costumes (women still wore panniers and men *tonnelet* skirts), the abolition of masks (then worn universally by all male dancers) to reveal the eloquent expressions he had marked on the features of Garrick; more variety in the compositions and less symmetry in the choreography, tragedy instead of frivolity as the theme – in short a realization of the power of ballet to 'speak to the heart'.

This was the first portent of the romantic movement. A return to nature was in the air; Rousseau's sentimental romance *La Nouvelle Héloise* appeared the same year. Noverre even argued against the (modified) 'turn-out' which was the basis of the classical technique. His teachings were enormously influential all over Europe. In Vienna Angiolini accused him of having stolen his ideas from Hilferding. But Hilferding was more of a neo-classicist, bent on a return to austere nobility; and the next great teacher was spiritually closer to him than to Noverre. His name was Carlo Blasis, and he worked mainly in Milan. While he was dancing in London as a young man of twenty-

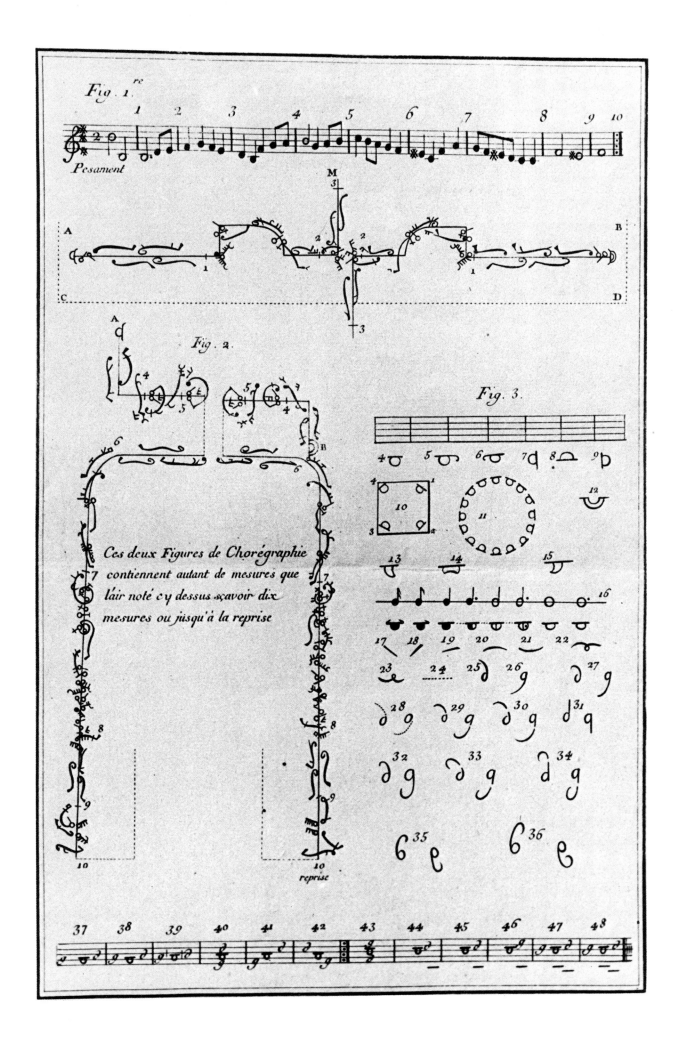

Above: formation for a horse ballet. Engraving by Stefano della Bella
Below: a dance phrase written in Labanotation, a system introduced by Rudolf von Laban in 1953. The movements read from the bottom upwards. This is part of the 'Violente' from the Prologue of 'The Sleeping Beauty', with Petipa's choreography

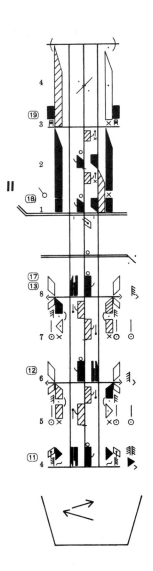

five, he wrote in 1820 a *Treatise on the Dance* which (together with *The Code of Terpsichore*, eight years later) approached the subject from a different angle – the point of view of technical training.

In 1837 Blasis was appointed head of the Imperial Academy of Dancing at the Scala, Milan. He proved to be a born teacher. Noverre's writings, much as he admired them, were, he thought, 'more adapted to instruct the professor than to improve the pupil'. He had a more limited but sharper vision; he studied the mechanics of the body with the single aim of producing the perfect classical dancer and devising harmonious compositions in which to display her or him. He was well educated in the arts (his sister was a prima donna at the Paris Opéra) and could quote from Dante or Tasso, Montesquieu or Leonardo. Like Noverre he took paintings and sculpture as his models. The new discoveries at Herculaneum inspired some of his groupings, and Raphael suggested poses. He devised a new attitude copied from the statue of Mercury by Bologna (still called the 'attitude') and invented a multitude of new steps – he was himself a strong technician – for his accomplished pupils. (He cheerfully talks of an *entrechat quatorze* – a sublime feat even today.) He was not only a clear thinker and writer but a practical trainer; he devised a system of exercises which have remained the basis of classical training ever since. In these he combined discipline with reason – he advised dancers to recognize the limitations of their physique – and he aimed consistently at balance and good taste. Even in this he was a moderate; he detested the 'broken wrist' which breaks the pure line of the arm, but also advised his pupils to 'throw a sort of abandon' into their positions; and he wrote that 'ballet should not be mere divertissements or dancing spectacles'.

This, unfortunately, is what they became, as the fame of his pupils spread across Europe and audiences encouraged their virtuosity. It was inevitable that a 'second Noverre' would arise, with a 'recall to nature'. This was Michel Fokine, the St Petersburg choreographer who was responsible for Diaghilev's first successes. He had little time to codify his beliefs until late in life, but in July 1914 he announced them, rather eccentrically, in the letter column of *The Times*. He laid down five principles – to make the form fit the subject, to avoid all irrelevant diversions, to replace conventional mime by natural gesture, to devise expressive groups instead of regimented patterns, and to blend dance, music and design into a single expressive whole.

The effects of Fokine's reforms (which were similar to those being put forward in drama in Russia and elsewhere) were manifest in Diaghilev's productions, particularly at the start. Later the romantic core around which they were built began to conflict with the more sophisticated views of the Paris avant-garde with which Diaghilev became associated, and the two men fell out. The classical-romantic dialectic continues today. If Balanchine ever writes a treatise it will surely oppose Fokine's doctrines – in brief comments he has already done so. Martha Graham has written rather more extensively, but more from a personal than a general angle. The 'next Noverre' is still in the wings.

One of the chief difficulties of compiling an instruction book in the early days of ballet was the absence of any technical terminology. This is how

Cornazano tried to explain in the fifteenth century what he meant by *maniera*:

> If you have the right foot to make a double step, you ought to balance on the left, which remains on the ground, turning your body slightly in that direction, and to undulate on the second step, raising yourself gently on this step, lowering yourself with equal gentleness on the third step which completes the double step.

A hundred and fifty years later Thoinot Arbeau, in his *Orchésographie* was making equally heavy weather of a simple *révérence* or bow:

> To perform the *révérence* you will keep the left foot firmly on the ground and, bending the right knee, carry the point of the toe a little to the rear of the left foot, at the same time doffing your bonnet or hat and saluting your damsel.

Two more Italians, Antonius de Arena and Fabrizio Caroso wrote similar prose descriptions of dance steps.

Clearly it would have been impossible to define the simplest group manoeuvres in this language. Some kind of sign system or notation, like that devised for music, was needed. It has been maintained that the Egyptians used hieroglyphs for this purpose, and that the Romans used shorthand signs for teaching social gestures; but convincing examples are missing. The first attempts at inventing a usable idiom appeared in the manuscripts of Guglielmo Ebreo, where we find a *révérence*, for instance marked simply by the letter 'r'.

Meanwhile, the invention of printing had given a tremendous boost to all methods of generally intelligible shorthand. Music notation made rapid strides, quickly outstripping dance in complication. It was not until 1699 that a French churchman called Raoul Feuillet published a book called *Choréographie ou l'Art de Décrire la Danse* in which – using a system invented shortly before by the dancer and Academy director Pierre Beauchamps – he (and Beauchamps' successor, Louis Pécour) set down a whole series of dances in use at the Paris Opera using curling designs and marks which indicate the pattern to be made by the dancers over the stage, with the accompanying music written above. This was the beginning of true dance notation.

It proved so useful and popular that he was able to bring out short brochures containing new dances every year, from 1703 till 1718, and it quickly spread to Germany, where it was used by Gottfried Taubert in Leipzig, and to England, where it appeared in 1735 in Kellom Tomlinson's *The Art of Dancing*. It was internationally intelligible because theatrical dance idioms were still based on the social dances – minuets, galliards or gavottes – which were familiar to any educated person. But ballet technique was developing rapidly. Costume reforms had made almost gymnastic movements possible. The turnout of the legs and feet – first prescribed by Arbeau in the sixteenth century – was increased from forty-five to ninety degrees. The newly fashionable shoes without heels enabled the girls to rise momentarily on the tips of their toes and to execute beats like a man. The old

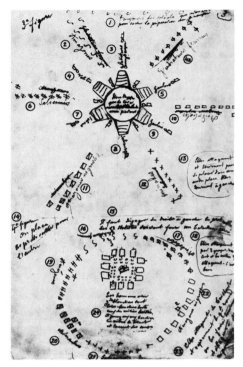

Above: a sketch from Marius Petipa's notes when planning 'The Sleeping Beauty' in St Petersburg, 1890

Below: an illustration from Carlo Blasis' *Treatise on the Dance*, 1820

system of notation was no longer adequate.

The analytical obsessions of the eighteenth century were a natural boost to the subject, which was discussed by Diderot (who came from the same town as Arbeau, Langres) in his famous *Encyclopédie*; but no workable solution was found. Carlo Blasis used a system of his own, and Bournonville used a mixture of plans and drawings in his notes. In 1852 Saint-Léon published his *Sténochoreographie* which involved adding an extra line to the musical stave, with pin-figures in it. Petipa employed diagrams and little 'stick figures' (as well as tiny models) when planning his elaborate ballets. The first real step towards a more rational system was taken by Vladimir Stepanov, a teacher at the Maryinsky school in St Petersburg, who in 1892 published a book called *Alphabet of Human Movements*. For this he used a nine-line stave with diagrams above – a comprehensive system which was actually taught for some time in the school and which he used to record over thirty current ballets. It was these records which Nicholas Sergueeff brought out of Russia in 1918 and which became the foundation of the Petipa classics in the west. Massine has further developed them in his own system.

In this century radically new approaches have been made to the problem, which seems on the point of being solved as satisfactorily as music-notation (which is itself, of course, far from perfect). In 1928 a Scottish dancer, Margaret Morris, published her own method: but it was overshadowed by Rudolf Laban's *Kinetographie*, issued the same year in Vienna. This is a very thorough system, which uses a three-line vertical stave, with symbols on each side of it, and has been much used in America where, in 1953, it was christened Labanotation. Another system invented in France by Pierre Conte uses a nine-line stave.

A different system – slightly simpler but far quicker, was devised in 1955 by Joan and Rudolf Benesh in London. It uses a five-line horizontal stave for each dancer or group and can be written down very rapidly by trained 'choreologists', as they are called. Though somewhat less comprehensive than Labanotation, it is much more practical, and has been adopted by several companies in Britain, Germany, Holland and Australia. There is also a mathematical notation-system, worked out in Israel by Noa Eshkol and Abraham Wachmann.

The very nature of movement means that it can never be completely recorded; the nearest attempts can only be the simulations adopted by Isaac Newton in his 'differential calculus'. This technique – the replacement of motion by a series of sequential 'stills' – is exactly the method of the cinema and the videotape. Nowadays, by collating a dance-film on tape with the relevant notation as close a record can be traced as following an opera performance with a music score. As more and more of these documents become available, dance will become open to real analysis, research and history – a development likely to affect both the nature of dance-theatre and of its status in the general cultural scene.

Above: an example of the idealized classical movements – impossible actually to achieve – on which Carlo Blasis based his teaching system. From *Treatise on the Dance*, 1820

Opposite: the opening of Juliet's solo in MacMillan's 'Romeo and Juliet' in Benesh notation

Juliet's Solo

XXI Design and Effects

The history of ballet design has followed two circular tracks: one is the same as that of the theatre in general – from primitive makeshift to elaborate extravagance and back; the other is more specialized, the trend from the architect-engineer to the painter-designer and back to constructions and effects.

Salvador Dali's design for Massine's 'Tristan Fou', with Ethery Pagava and André Eglevsky. Presented by the Grand Ballet de Monte-Carlo in 1949

The earliest 'stages' in Egyptian times were the forecourts of temples and tombs, and in ancient Greece the round 'orchestrae' or dancing-grounds were traditionally adapted from threshing floors. Only in later periods was the performer's changing tent or 'skena' decorated to present an entrance or exit. It was soon replaced by a permanent stone structure and the elaboration of the theatre building began to necessitate something more flexible; by the third century BC the gigantic theatre at Megalopolis, which seated over twenty thousand spectators was equipped with a wooden stage, complete with the usual side pavilions or *paraskenoi*, which was rolled in and out on wheels. By the second century AD the Romans were using an enormous *scaenae frons*, usually in the form of a central doorway with side niches, such as that at Sabratha in North Africa; painted panels were sometimes set behind the openings.

After the fall of Rome, when dance had to make a new start in Northern Europe, a different approach began. This was the tradition of decorated floats or waggons, each forming a tiny portable stage; they were pulled on and off to make a series of episodes in a kind of pageant. In the wealthy Renaissance courts in Italy these developed into *trionfi* and *intermezzi* (diversions during a play or banquet) of spectacular splendour. (Mantegna's painting 'Parnassus' in the Louvre museum in Paris gives a good idea of the effect.) Soon the little sets were placed on the ground as temporary scenery or props. The famous *Balet Comique de la Royne* had two of these miniature scenes, one each side of a raised platform stage. But emphasis at this time was primarily on the costumes, whose extravagance stressed the importance of the aristocratic performer; movement was limited and the decoration was rich, heavy and detailed.

The development of the proscenium theatre in Italy permitted huge new strides in stage design. In 1490 Leonardo had been limited to costumes and floats – though later he also dreamed up a revolving stage – but in 1518 Raphael was painting a whole front curtain for a performance (of *I Suppositani*) before the Pope. Productions quickly became extremely elaborate, and were recorded not only in engravings but in several printed books.

The earliest of these is by Sebastiano Serlio, a Bolognese painter who was engaged by François I to help decorate his palace at Fontainebleau. In 1545 he published in *Le second Livre de la Perspective*, a section of his 'Architettura', some detailed instructions for the stage design based on Vitruvius's principles. He recommended a fairly steeply raked stage (a gradient of one in nine), made 'even and strong to accommodate the dancers'.

In Florence the chief designer at this time was Bernardo Buontalenti, who developed with gusto the possibilities of illusion offered by the science of perspective – an ideal device for an audience with a fixed viewpoint which he carried out in every detail, from wings of diminishing size to graded performers, with children at the back to suggest full size people in the

A movable stage prop for use in a ballet involving both horsemen and dancers. From the Pageant in honour of Duke Johann Friedrich von Württemberg, Stuttgart, 1616. Engraving by Matthäus Merian

distance. He was succeeded by Giulio Parigi, whose spectacular effects deeply impressed a young Englishman travelling in Italy, Inigo Jones. On his return to London Jones developed them in a series of brilliant 'masques' over a period of thirty-five years. Parigi's son Alfonso succeeded him, but he was outshone by a Venetian designer, Giacomo Torelli, who added to accurate perspective effects ingenious mechanical devices such as linked stage wings which could be changed simultaneously by a single manipulator. In 1654 he was summoned to Paris by Louis XIV, where he mounted some of the most splendid of the spectacular *ballets de cour*.

Meanwhile another pupil of Parigi, Joseph Furttenbach, had published in 1645, soon after his return to his native Germany, a section of a book called *Architettura Recreationis* which set out instructions both for building and setting a stage and for lighting it and the auditorium (not to be darkened for another 150 years). His imaginary stage was not large. He suggested a 36 ft opening narrowing to 18 ft at the back, with a vertiginous rake – nearly one in five – to its 30 ft depth, and he allowed 2 ft 6 in. for a pit along the front – 'an excellent position for the musicians'. He also prescribed for the audience, advising: 'Care must be taken to put the most beautiful ladies in the middle.' The aim was to inspire the performers with more zest.

By now the curtain in front of the stage was drawn up slowly at the start of the performance to surprise the audience with scenic splendours, instead of being dropped down abruptly as before.

Lighting played a vital part in these spectacles, with fireworks going off above the fountains and special effects obtained by mirrors and reflectors and

164

jars of coloured water in front of the lights. Furttenbach was dubious about the efficacy of footlights, since the evil-smelling smoke obscured as much as the candles and oil-lamps illuminated, and he devised special ways of fixing lights so that they did not collapse when the dancing began, 'which brings discredit to the stage manager'.

Another Italian writer, Nicola Sabbatini, gave similar practical advice in his *Manual for Constructing Theatrical Scenes* of 1638, which vividly conveys the very live nature òf theatre at that time. The favourite scenes were heaven and hell, storms and catastrophes. Heaven, the abode of classical gods, was an occasion for sliding cut-out clouds and the gloria, a platform on which gods could descend with the aid of pulleys. Catastrophes offered even more scope to the engineer-designer; with revolving cloths giving the effect of heaving waves, thunder obtained by rolling a stone ball across the theatre ceiling, and red lamps illuminating the snapping jaws of hell. Realism was carried to great lengths when a conflagration was required: 'A little before the appointed time, soak pieces of cloth in aqua vitae . . . and quickly fix them upon the faces of the houses which are to be affected. When the time comes, one man is deputed to each house. With a taper he sets fire to the face, and the turning of the triangles sets fire to all the houses and completes the operation.' (The 'triangles' were three-sided wings, or *periaktoi*, which could be revolved to present different scenes.) Sabbatini added cautiously: 'There will always be a certain risk,' and this was made all the more acute by the voluminous costumes worn by both sexes.

A Jesuit father, Père Menestrier, writing in 1682 in his *Des Ballets Anciens et Modernes* laid down the established styles for the equally established characters, ranging from Romans (whose short skirts were favoured by the men, as they gave more freedom to move) Greeks, Persians, Moors, Turks and Indians. The supporting cast would include Satyrs, Rivers (with waterpots), Zephyrs (with bellows), the Seasons, Virtues, Day and Night, and sundry arts, occupations and sciences with appropriate symbols worked into expensive dresses. These became particularly handsome under Louis XIV in Paris, where Jean Bérain, Claude Gillot and Jean Baptiste Martin invented hundreds of exquisite costumes for the elaborate *ballets de cour*, which became more and more exaggerated as the years passed. Around 1718 the girls began to wear wide pannier skirts and the men countered with similar *tonnelets*. In 1730 Camargo shortened her skirts to reveal her footwork and began to wear knickers beneath them – an important step for choreographers – while at the same time Marie Sallé heralded the neo-classical style with her simple transparent dresses.

In the austere sets needed for the heroic ballets of this genre a less fanciful and more realistic note was struck, partly influenced by Noverre's reforming lectures. The neo-classical age at the start of the nineteenth century demanded severe, crisply defined settings with an emphasis on linear architecture. Tricks and surprise effects had less place in these dramas and the age of the architect-engineer who had so far dominated theatre designs began to fade away. He was replaced in the Romantic movement by the painter. Suggestion replaced illusion, and the broad evocative washes of the water-colourist supplanted the bright and confident visual statements of earlier

Project by Filippo Juvara for a set in the private theatre of Cardinal Ottaboni in the Palazzo della Cancelleria, Rome, *c.* 1710

MACHINE INVENTÉE PAR D'HERMAND

ages. For the next hundred years the tendency towards turning the stage into an animated easel picture was to grow in strength, culminating in the Diaghilev experiments in which dancers often became mere animated pictorial mobiles.

The first manifestation of the Romantic movement pointed the way. The settings for *La Sylphide* in 1832 were by Pierre Ciceri and the costumes by Eugène Lami, both trained as painters. The white full-skirted dresses – far removed from the modified day-dresses which had been the rule up to now – were to become a kind of uniform for ballerinas for over a century (the slippers with stiffened toes which crept into use at about this time marked another move away from everyday life and social dancing) and the picturesque scenery became a model for the three-hundred productions which Ciceri mounted for the opera during the next thirty years. As a nineteenth century artist he was much interested in light, and in 1822 he introduced gas lighting which, with its extra luminosity and easy control, proved a powerful influence on stage production; one of its by-products was the spotlight, which encouraged the star system. (It was to be replaced by electricity in the 1880s.)

Above: Pierre Ciceri's design for Act II of 'La Sylphide', presented at the Paris Opéra in 1832. His landscape decors, helped by the new gas lighting, contributed for a generation to the development of the Romantic ballet. The costumes were by Eugene Lami, though the design for the ballerina – the first white tutu ever – is mysteriously missing.

Opposite: stage 'flying machine', invented by d'Hermand for a ballet at the French court. Engraving, late 17th century

A design by 'C. Wilhelm' (William Pitcher) for a 'Swan Ballet' for the Alexandra Theatre, Liverpool, 1886

Opposite above: two flying machines, suspended on wires, serve as thrones for Juno and Ceres, in 'L'Educazione di Achille e delle Nereidi' in Turin Theatre, 1650

Opposite below: a genuine rhinoceros takes part in 'L'Unione per la Peregrina Margherita Reale e Celeste', presented at the Turin Theatre in 1660

With the growing importance of the scenery, the costumes became simpler, but, as the century progressed and productions became vulgarized, they began to compete in complication and splendour, with disastrously overloaded results. Luigi Manzotti's mammoth spectacles in Milan included regiments of brightly costumed extras, sometimes swelled by horses and even elephants. In London 'C. Wilhelm' at the Empire and N. Alias at the Alhambra vied with each other in fanciful extravaganzas in which symbolism and decoration were interwoven with the panache, but not the taste, of the Renaissance.

The almost single-handed reforms of Diaghilev at the beginning of the twentieth century have passed – significantly – into the history of painting as well as into the story of the theatre. He had started as an art-connoisseur and organizer and he conceived the idea of employing easel painters to devise a new idea for each ballet instead of the old system of adapting conventional set pieces. At first he used Russians like Alexandre Benois, Leon Bakst, Nikolai Roerich, Nathalia Goncharova and Mikhail Larionov who were familiar with ballet and who subjected themselves easily to theatrical collaboration. Some of his later Parisian contributors, such as Derain and Matisse, also accommodated themselves without difficulty to the role of decorators; but others, like Rouault, Miró and in particular the forceful Picasso, seized on the stage with glee as an extension of their painting. The development culminated in *Parade* in 1917, in which some of the dancers were completely encased in immovable structures made according to the conventions of painting rather than of dance. Fernand Léger's vivid designs for *La Création du Monde*, which were carried out in 1923 for de Maré's Ballets Suédois, attempted a somewhat similar translation of pictorial conventions into stage effects.

The introduction of the artist into stage decoration had a wonderfully stimulating effect. Painters like Matisse, Dufy and Dali contributed some striking ballet designs in the 1930s, and after World War I France produced a painterly designer in the person of Christian Bérard. But a reaction was bound to set in. The American choreographer Merce Cunningham has brilliantly followed Diaghilev's custom of using gallery artists instead of theatre designers; but he has picked those who avoid straight easel paintings in their normal work. Artists like Robert Rauschenberg, Jasper Johns, Robert Morris and Andy Warhol devised contributions which were an integral part of the action rather than passive settings. The sculptor Noguchi has made combinations of props, sets and sculpture for Martha Graham, and some American artists have actually taken part in performances.

All this forms part of a tendency towards the rejection of ballet design as an extension of painting and a reversion to a much earlier tradition in which the designer was either limited merely to providing costumes (as in many Balanchine ballets) or else to devise lighting, props or solid space-creating constructions, in which architecture plays a larger part than drawing or painting. It is significant that two of the most successful contemporary designers for opera-house stages, Josef Swoboda and Nicholas Georgiadis, were both trained as architects. The tradition of painterly ballet designers survives most strongly in Paris where it first began, often with an emphasis on

L'HVMOR SANGVIGNO AEREO.

Above: scene for 'La Primavera Trionfante dell' Inverno' in the Turin Theatre, choreographed by Filippo d'Aglié, 1657
Left: the costume for 'L'Humor Sanguigno Aereo' in 'Il Carnevale Languente', serves as prototype for later characters, such as the Bluebird in 'The Sleeping Beauty'

Above: design by Sanquirico for Sal-
vatore Vigano's ballet 'L'Alunno della
Giumenta' ('The Mare's Pupil'), Scala
Theatre, Milan, 1812. Engraving

Right: set by Alessandro Sanquirico for
'Il Naufragio di La Peyrouse', a ballet
by William Barrymore at the Canob-
biana Theatre, Milan, 1825. Engraving

Overleaf: Two centuries of ballet fashion – an enchaînement of characteristic
costumes decade by decade from the
1770s to the 1970s. Drawing by Mark
Wheeler

1770s

1780s

1790s

1800s

1910s

1900s

1890

1920s

1930s

1940s

1810s

1820s

1830s

1840s

1850s

1860s

1870s

1880s

1950s

1960s

1970s

Mark Wheeler 1976

Right: Bakst's design for Potiphar in Fokine's 'La Légende de Joseph', which he designed for Diaghilev in 1914. The sets were by Jose-Maria Sert, and the principal part was Massine's first important role

Opposite: two of Christian Bérard's costumes for Balanchine's 'Cotillon', a romantic ballet presented by Colonel de Basil's Ballet Russe in 1932

Dessin de Léon BAKST

Right: the abstract backcloth by the Spanish painter Joan Mirò for 'Jeux d'Enfants', choreographed by Massine for Colonel de Basil's Ballet Russe in 1932

Below: Derek Jarman's setting for Frederick Ashton's 'Jazz Calendar', presented by the Royal Ballet in 1968: Friday's Children (Antoinette Sibley and Rudolf Nureyev)

Opposite: Nureyev dives through the backcloth at the end of Act I of Roland Petit's 'Paradise Lost' for the Royal Ballet, 1966. The designer was the French painter Martial Raysse

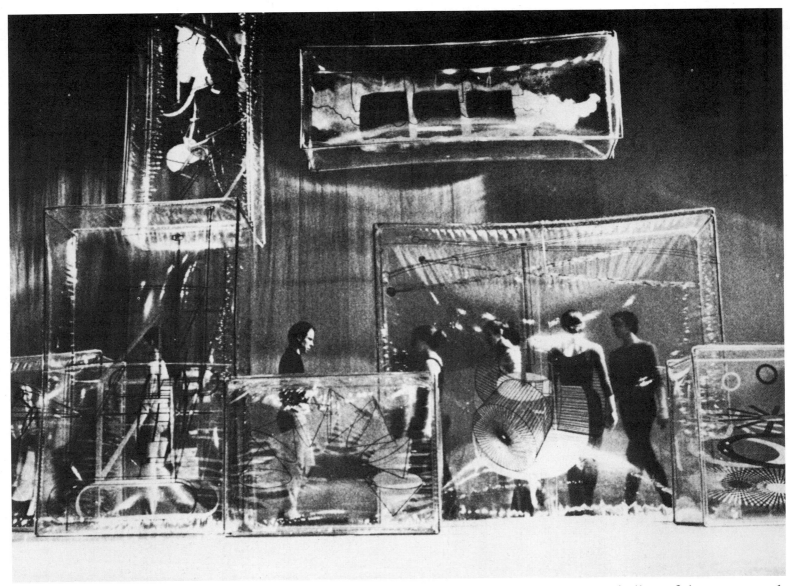

Above: one of the designs by avant-garde artists used by Merce Cunningham for his company 'Walkaround Time', 1968. This setting for 'Walkaround Time', 1968, is based on Marcel Duchamps' painting 'The Large Glass or the Bride Stripped bare by her Bachelors'

Opposite: A. E. Volinin as The Bluebird in a Moscow production of 'The Sleeping Beauty', about 1920. The large wings must have dictated slower arm movements than are now usual in the West, where most modern designers dispense with the wings altogether

spectacular fantasy, which harks back to the court ballets of the seventeenth century.

Design is an unescapable attribute to dance in ballet; music can be dispensed with, but even nudity on a bare stage – the extreme modern reaction to over-decoration – is a form of visual presentation. How it will develop in the future depends on many things – economics, social patterns and theatre planning as well as trends in art and, of course, dance. It is now a subject for serious research and sophisticated training in many countries, and the advantages of employing artists from outside the theatre are reduced. It seems likely that the movement away from painted illusion will persist for a time: if Diaghilev were alive today he might be looking at aircraft design or computers. But the demand for economy and flexibility may check it. The balance between mechanical and pictorial character and period, kinetics and visual delight is constantly being readjusted in a process in which there are no rules except the one which lays down inexorably that what looks right is right.

XXII 'Sleeping Beauties'

Below:
1890 Maryinsky Theatre, St
Petersburg
Director: Petipa
Costumes: Vsevolojsky
Sets: Levogt (Prologue),
Andreev (Act I), Botcharov
(Act II – Vision-scene by
Ivanov), Shishkov (Act III
and Apotheosis)
Massive and handsome,
especially Shishkov's outdoor
Act III

Opposite top:
1921 Alhambra Theatre, London
Director: Nikolai Sergueyev
Costumes and sets: Bakst
Opulent and colourful, based on
Bibiena and the Louis XIV
period

Opposite bottom:
1946 Covent Garden, London
Director: Ninette de Valois
Costumes and sets: Oliver
Messel
Light and lyrical, with Louis XV
as the dominant influence

Ever since Charles Perrault wrote the story in 1697, *The Sleeping Beauty* has attracted theatre librettists. It was first made into ballet in 1829, when Jean Aumer mounted a version at the Paris Opéra, with a score by Hérold (the design has disappeared). It was quite successful, but it has been overshadowed by the Petipa-Tchaikovsky version launched in St Petersburg in 1890, which became a classic overnight. It would seem hard to modify; both the action and the period are firmly laid down in the libretto, and the composer clearly delineates the mood. Yet already it has undergone many variations, each of which reveals the taste of its particular place, public and period – the changing face of a persistent dream.

Six versions of Act III are shown here.

Right:
1952 Kirov Theatre, Leningrad
 Director: Konstantin Sergueyev
 Costumes and sets: Simon
   Virsaladze
 Spare and spacious, with the
   accent on lyricism

Opposite top:
1960 Champs Elysées Theatre, Paris
 Directors: Nijinska and
   Helpmann
 Costumes and sets: Raymundo
   de Larrain
 Fantasy takes the place of
   period accuracy

Opposite bottom:
1966 La Scala, Milan
 Director: Nureyev
 Costumes and sets: Nicholas
   Georgiadis
 Grand and sumptuous, a return
   to the Louis XIV tradition

XXIII The Music

Music and dance have always been linked in the most intimate of embraces: but in their theatrical manifestation they eventually branched out in different directions, owing to the separate demands of movement and song. Slowly productions split into successive episodes in which one or the other were featured exclusively.

This system survived until very recent times. In Renaissance entertainments the dancers still had their own director and their own orchestra. The ballet-master was expected to be expert at music as well as dance. Beaujoyeulx was responsible for the score as well as the choreography for *Le Balet Comique de la Royne* in 1581, and when the twenty-year-old Giacomo Battista Lulli arrived in Paris in 1620 and became Jean-Baptiste Lully, he was engaged by Louis XIV as a violinist as well as a dancer.

He became a key figure in dance history. With his talent, charm and push he quickly became a favourite of the fifteen-year-old king, and his composition of the *Ballet de la Galanterie du Temps* confirmed him as a composer. He acquired his own sixteen-player orchestra, known as 'Les Petits Violons' and devised a number of successful entertainments in which both he and the king took part. In 1664 he began a collaboration with Molière which culminated in *Le Bourgeois Gentilhomme*, and in 1672 he acquired control of the new Académie Royale de Musique which had been founded three years before to encourage 'opera and drama in music and French verse on the Italian model'. In his years as director his productions in this style – mixtures of singing and pantomime with short dance numbers – were so successful that ballet insertions became a traditional and even compulsory element in operas produced in Paris for the next two hundred years. Jean-Philippe Rameau, one of his first successors, continued the idiom in a slightly heavier style, his most lasting production being *Les Indes Galantes* of 1738, which included a whole act, *Les Sauvages*, devoted to dancing.

Charles II of England had been much impressed by Lully's productions when he was in Paris and even sent a musician over from London to study them. Their influence was evident in works like John Blow's 'masque for dancing', *Venus and Adonis*, of 1687 and Purcell's *Fairy Queen* of 1692, which contained many dance numbers. In Vienna the distinguished Kapellmeister Christoph Gluck began to make similar opera ballets in the Hoftheater of a less frivolous character. His *Don Juan* of 1761 was a serious mime-drama with thirty short dance episodes of an almost symphonic nature. They were choreographed by Gasparo Angiolini, for whom he composed several more ballets, and he later worked with Noverre in Paris.

Noverre also introduced at the Paris opera another celebrated Austrian composer, Mozart, from whom in 1778 he commissioned a new score for *Les Petits Riens*, a ballet which he had already tried out in Vienna with a different composer. It was reasonably successful, receiving six performances, but Mozart grumbled to his father that he had only done it out of friendship for Noverre, adding: 'I absolutely will not do anything if I don't know in advance what I am to get for it.' Another ballet score, *L'Epreuve d'Amour* is also credited to Mozart, but its authenticity is doubtful.

Vienna was the scene of another ballet collaboration by a famous

An impression by Valentine Gross of Maria Piltz as the Chosen Virgin in Nijinsky's 'Le Sacre du Printemps', 1913. The musical phrase from Stravinsky's score which it illustrates is bar 218 of the piano score

Jean-Baptiste Lully (or Lulli), born in Italy, joined the court of Louis XIV as a dancer, turned to composing, and quickly became the Director of the Académie Royal de Musique. A man of immense energy and prodigal talent, he composed many ballets and operas and was a powerful influence in turning the old mixed-media court entertainments into more specialized art forms, in which music counted for more than speech, and either dance or singing predominated

composer. In 1801 a score was commissioned from Beethoven for a ballet in honour of the Empress Maria Theresa, *The Creatures of Prometheus*. The libretto and choreography were by Salvatore Vigano. As a young man Beethoven had already written (as 'ghost' for a Bonn nobleman) a suite of eight dance numbers called *Ritterballett*. He conceived the Promethean legend in typically heroic terms, seeing the hero as the liberator of mankind; a theme from the apotheosis was to reappear in his 'Eroica' symphony. A dance episode of a less solemn nature appeared in Vienna about twenty years later, with the now well-known ballet music from Schubert's *Rosamund, Princess of Cyprus*.

By now opera had decisively separated from ballet and obviously offered far more scope to the serious composer. But right through the nineteenth century French opera-composers, from Auber to Gounod, contributed a dance divertissement to every production, and their foreign colleagues followed suit. Meyerbeer's dances in *Robert le Diable* were inadvertently to become the springboard for the whole Romantic movement in ballet and he introduced a roller-skating number into *Le Prophète* in 1849; Rossini – who detested ballet and even composed satirical pieces with names like *Valse Antidansante* – inserted a pas-de-six and some Tyrolean dances into his *William Tell* and Wagner dutifully added the Venusberg dance numbers to *Tannhäuser*. In 1887 a ballet was even incongruously enlivening Verdi's *Otello*.

The French composer who seemed best equipped to be a ballet composer, Hector Berlioz, unluckily limited himself in this idiom to the carnival in *Benvenuto Cellini* and the over-elaborate 'Royal Hunt and Storm' scene in *Les Troyens*. It was not until 1870 that Léo Delibes emerged with a sparkling score which has lent longevity to a rather childish ballet *Coppélia*, afterwards composing a charming pastiche in the old, classical style, *Sylvia*.

In other countries dance-music was playing a similar subordinate role to opera. Johann Strauss in Austria, Richard Strauss in Germany and Smetana in Prague all devised short but lively dance numbers for their operas. Russian composers, with their exceptional national sense of rhythm, were particularly fertile. Glinka, Borodin, Rimsky-Korsakov and Mussorgsky could all have turned their talents successfully to ballet, and in 1877 Piotr Tchaikovsky's *Swan Lake* revealed at a stroke a composer who seemed designed by nature to write for dancing. His other full-length ballets, *The Sleeping Beauty* and *The Nutcracker*, confirmed his unique sympathy for movement – a gift which is illustrated by the fact that many of his concert compositions have proved almost equally effective as a basis for dancing.

It is Russians who have dominated the ballet orchestra-pit ever since. Alexander Glazunov carried on the rich tradition of Tchaikovsky in St Petersburg. The sharp ear of Diaghilev – whose first inclination had been towards music – spotted the potentialities of Igor Stravinsky when he heard one of his first compositions, *Fireworks*, in 1909, and immediately commissioned *The Firebird* from him. Stravinsky subsequently devoted a large slice of his output to ballet in works like *Petrushka, Le Sacre du Printemps, Apollo* and *Les Noces* for Diaghilev; and, later, *Orpheus* and *Agon* for Balanchine, with whom he worked very closely in America.

Meanwhile in Russia Sergei Prokofiev was proving adept at a form which Stravinsky never ever attempted, the full-length narrative ballet. He had already composed some short ballets (including *The Prodigal Son*) for Diaghilev; after returning to Russia he produced three highly successful long works, *Romeo and Juliet, Cinderella* and *The Stone Flower*. Dmitri Shostakovitch could clearly also have been a great composer for dance if he had wished, but he never wrote a ballet; however he consented to several of his concert works being used for dancing, and the results make his decision all the more regrettable.

The internationally minded Diaghilev had commissioned ballets from musicians from many countries, including several French composers, Claude Debussy (*Jeux*), Ravel (*Daphnis and Chloë*), Francis Poulenc (*Les Biches*) and Erik Satie (*Parade, Mercure* and *Relâche*), and Manuel de Falla (*The Three Cornered Hat*) from Spain. In Hungary, Béla Bartók composed two fine one-act ballet scores, the poetic *The Wooden Prince* and the violently decadent *The Miraculous Mandarin*, which was not surprisingly never performed until after his death. Among other distinguished composers who have written for ballet are the American Aaron Copland (*Appalachian Spring*), the British Ralph Vaughan Williams (*Job*), William Walton (*Façade*) and Benjamin Britten (*The Prince of the Pagodas*), and the German Hans Werner Henze (*Tancredi* and *Ondine*). The last two composers have tackled the most difficult form, which has daunted many composers as well as choreographers, the full-length ballet.

With Isadora Duncan leading the way, choreographers in this century have felt free to plunder any existing music as an accompaniment to dance. The result has greatly benefited ballet, extending its range and provoking new movements and structures, and also suggesting new relationships between the score and the dancing. As a rule they are still usually tied very closely; but experiments have been made (especially by Merce Cunningham with John Cage) in a looser relationship, in which the music is simply laid alongside the movement, like a film score against a film. (Nijinsky's *L' Après-midi d'un Faune* was one of the first ballets to set music and movement in contrast instead of in harmony.)

The unabashed expropriation of music never intended for ballet has led to some abuse and justified protest, but also to many outstanding successes. Much controversy arose in the 1930s when Massine composed several ballets to symphonies by Tchaikovsky, Brahms and Beethoven. (The eminent British music-critic Ernest Newman unexpectedly sprang to his defence.) It was not in fact an entirely new practice: Beethoven's Pastoral Symphony had been used for ballet several times since 1829, and ever since choreographers have felt free to dip freely into any source, even spoken poetry – or silence.

These experiments have helped to clarify the qualifications of a good ballet score. It needs to be rhythmically lively and varied (most concert-hall scores are built on rhythmic patterns sustained too long for ballet); exceptionally fertile invention (for physical reasons dance moves in very short measures, demanding new themes at a rate few composers can keep up); it is best when the movement seems inherent in the phrase (experienced composers like Ludwig Minkus, the Viennese-Hungarian composer who worked in Russia

Igor Stravinsky, *c.* 1913. The many ballets he composed, first for Diaghilev and later for Balanchine, set new standards for dance music, and indirectly influenced the development of dance itself

Serge Prokofiev, photographed when he was working with Diaghilev in Paris, *c.* 1925

with Petipa, was exceptionally adept at this); and ideally it should contain the mysterious and impalpable quality which makes it come alive on the stage. The impact of unassuming scores like those of Minkus or Adam's *Giselle*, or superficially dry reserved ones like Stravinsky's *Agon*, prove that composing for ballet presents a problem as difficult as those of any other form of music-making; the rarity of successes suggests that the gift of solving it is granted to few. Many gifted opera composers, such as Verdi, have proved very mediocre when it comes to writing music for dance, and the quality which distinguishes strong dramatic music from good theatre music – a very different thing – is mysterious. Bach, for instance, seems to be easily adaptable for dance and even (as in *Le Jeune Homme et la Mort*) spine-chilling on stage, while Beethoven, apparently more emotional, has proved resistant to most choreographers. Wagner seems inappropriate to dance, while Mahler blends easily with it.

Acknowledgements

I have consulted too many books in compiling this one to make any bibliography meaningful, but I readily acknowledge my debt to previous researchers. I would like to thank the curators and staff of the collections which have responded to my requests for pictures, and the photographers who have willingly looked out material. I owe a particular debt to Parmenia Migel-Ekstrom both for permission to reproduce pictures from her collection and for passing her expert and observant eye over the text; any errors, however, are my own. I must also especially thank Mr Bamber Gascoigne for making available the photographs taken by Christina Gascoigne of the Turin Ballet; Mr Ivor Guest for answering enquiries about the nineteenth century; Mr John Cavanagh of Mottisfont Abbey for his help in allowing pictures to be photographed from his collection; Mr Robin Wright and Miss Jeanne Griffiths of London Editions for understanding and professional support; and my wife for sustained assistance and toleration.

Alexander Bland, 1976

Index

PICTURE CREDITS AND SOURCES